THE
EVERYBODY
IS BORN
EQUAL

DICTIONARY

DALE TROMBLEY

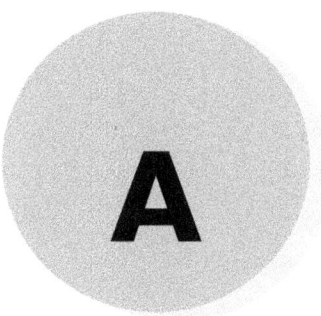

A—The best or highest quality or rank. Some people think they are this but according to God everybody is equal.

Aardvark—The aardvark is an ugly pig like animal but it eats ants. So if you go on a picnic and don't want to be bothered by ants, take an aardvark along. Just close your eyes when you eat and he won't spoil your appetite.

Abacus—Bring back the use of hands and brain more, and you will be a smarter and more productive human being.

Abandon—Never give up anything, unless it is a bad habit.

Abate—Put an end to sin and watch the saints marching in.

Abbey—The monks in monasteries give up the luxuries of life to pray for a better life for us all.

Abbreviate—Some people should shorten their mouth span.

ABC—Don't let watching too much television distract your children from learning the rudiments of arithmetic, reading and writing.

Abdicate—I don't think anybody should give up a crown unless it gives him or her pain, yet Christ didn't give up on his crown, and it gave him pain.

Abdomen—Be careful what you put in your stomach. Your health depends upon what you eat. Eat wise and you stay wise.

Abduct—Never carry off by force or kidnap somebody unless leaving the person or child where you abducted them will cause harm to them.

Abed—Never be in bed with the wrong person or for the wrong reason unless it is your husband or wife.

Abet—Don't abet somebody in the commission of a crime unless you like jail time.

Abeyance—It's all right to set aside some of your ideas for future reference as long as they don't become permanent dust collectors.

Abhor—To hate. Never hate anybody or anything unless it is dangerous to your health. Love is so much better.

Abide—Accept the consequences of your actions, but don't let your free will suffer because of it.

Ability—Talents. Some people have few and some people have many. No matter how few or how many you have, be thankful. It is the quality of talents that counts, not the quantity.

Ablaze—Let your heart be radiant with love for your fellowmen.

Able—Having the power to do something. Some people can do many things at a time. Some people can't chew gum and walk at the same time. Who cares? Just as long as you are satisfied with what you can do.

Able-bodied—If you are this, help those who aren't.

Abnormal—Different. Enjoy it. God made everybody and everything different. So accept the difference and work for a better world for all mankind and all things of nature.

Aboard—Come aboard God's ship, it will be well worth the journey.

Abolish—Don't abolish anything you will regret ending later.

Abolition—Slavery was supposed to be done away with, but the way some people have to work, it makes you wonder.

Abominable snowman—Some people report for work looking like this. They should look into a mirror before they go out of their house.

Abortion—A tough issue. Every case is different. Let God be the judge of who was right or wrong.

About—If everybody went about their own business in this world, we wouldn't have so many noses stuck where they don't belong.

About-face—Don't be afraid to change your mind, especially if you are sinning.

Above—Where God is supposed to be, but He is everywhere.

Aboveboard—Be up front with your dealings, and people will know honesty is part of you.

Aboveground—Better to keep your feet above ground. You will get your fill of below ground after you are dead.

Abracadabra—Don't you wish by saying this word you could bring peace to the whole world.

Abrasive—Don't be this to a wrong person; otherwise people might call you sandpaper-face when this person gets done with you.

Abreast—Keep up to date of the latest news and developments of the world, and you won't need an encyclopedia to refresh your memory. You will be one.

Abridge—Don't abridge your life by smoking, drinking, or taking drugs. Your life could be a long novel.

Abroad—Remember to behave yourself and act your age when you are abroad. You are a reflection of your country. Think of the men and women who died for your country. Do yourself and their memory proud.

Abrupt—Some people act this way. Don't let it get to you. The less you let people bother you, the more easily you will make it through life.

Absent—Don't be away from your children too long. An absentee parent leads to a child who does not know what the true love of a parent is.

Absentee ballot—The best way to vote. Take a trip to a foreign country during the election and you don't have to listen to the hot air and mudslinging at home.

Absent-Minded—If this happens to you a lot, get help, because in today's world your full attention is needed to make it through the night.

Absent without leave—Sometimes home is more important and awaits you.

Absolute—One hopes everyone is whole in body and soul. If you are not, do the best that you can with what you have.

Absolution—A wonderful gift, but don't repeat the sin; absolution may not be so easy to obtain the next time.

Absorb—Soak up all you can in your mind; it may not be as much as the next person can absorb, but at least it's something you can recall for future use.

Abstinence—Refraining from liquor is fine, but a drink once in a while doesn't hurt some people. Just don't take too many drinks and drive.

Abstract—Not easy to understand, but it breaks up the boredom of life once in a while.

Absurd—Some things are silly and ridiculous, but that makes the world go around.

Abundance—Share your wealth with poor people.

Abuse—Report it if you see or suspect it. No person or animal should have to take it. Even the abuse of someone else's property is wrong and should be reported.

Abuzz—This happens when too many mouths get together at the same place.

Abyss—Don't be afraid of the deep, because with God's help you can overcome anything.

Academic freedom—Okay as long as students are allowed to think for themselves and are able to sort out what is right or wrong.

Academy—A good place to learn to achieve a common goal with others. The goal being to broaden one's knowledge.

Acapulco—A city in southern Mexico on the Pacific Ocean. It is a popular resort with a fine natural harbor surrounded by cliffs and high ridges of land or rocks jutting out into the body of water. People dive off the cliffs here. Be careful if you dive off a cliff, that you don't hit your head on part of a cliff or a rock in the water. Better to have lots of experience before you try it.

Acapulco gold—Slang for Mexican-grown marijuana that is considered to be very strong. Know what you are doing before you try it. Don't try it and drive a car. Also, don't walk across a street when you try it. You might get hit by a car or people might think you are jaywalking.

Accelerate—Increase the speed with which your heart meets the need of others.

Accent—We may speak differently, but we are all after the same thing: to make it through the night.

Accept—Accept what you can. What you can't accept, try to cope with the best you can.

Access—It would be wonderful if we could have the keys to some people's minds so that they could be helped.

Accessible—Don't be this to strangers until you know them better.

Accessory—If you play this game with a lawbreaker, be ready to play a new kind of game if you get caught: the behind-the-bars game.

Access road—Make sure the access road of your life leads to a brighter future for yourself.

Accident—Don't fret over things that weren't your fault.

Accident Insurance—Good to have but it won't heal the loss of a loved one.

Accident-prone—Don't let being accident-prone stop you from living. When you stop living you quit being you, and being you is more important than being accident-prone.

Acclaim—Give praise to another person whenever she or he deserves it—even a child who tries hard and still receives an F on his or her report card or finishes last in a race.

Accommodate—Do as many favors and services as you can for the needy and elderly.

Accommodation—When you are traveling, find the best motel or hotel you can to stay overnight in. You need the best rest you can get because driving and falling asleep at the wheel is dangerous.

Accompanist—This person may seem second fiddle to some people, but first fiddle couldn't get off the ground without the support of this person.

Accompany—Attend an event with somebody who is lonely.

Accomplice—Don't be one of these, because if you are caught, bars become your constant companions.

Accomplish—Do what you can in one day, but don't tire yourself out. Tomorrow is another day.

Accord—I wish all countries could step in agreement with one another. What a safe world it would be for all God's children.

Accordion—Some people call this the squeeze box. I call it the sweet box because of all the sweet sounding music that comes out of it.

Account—Don't be afraid to take notice of your mistakes. We learn from them. Account for them and get on with your life.

Accountable—Be responsible when your duties require it, and people will look upon you as a person who can give a good account of oneself.

Accountant—A good professional because he or she helps people to balance their lifestyle.

Accredit—If you are appointed as an ambassador to a foreign country, make sure you make your country proud. Behave yourself and don't throw any wild parties.

Accreditation—Let's hope all schools gain this.

Accumulate—If you pile up lots of material goods, share them with others who need them.

Accurate—Don't be afraid of making errors. Only God is errorless.

Accursed—You are never doomed even if there is only one ray of hope left. Prayers always help too.

Accuse—Don't point fingers unless your own slate is clean.

Accustom—Don't become so accustomed to someone that you don't appreciate them for what they are: a child of God.

Ace—Be an expert at bringing joy to others.

Ace in the hole—It's okay to hold your advantage in reserve but not so long that it becomes a disadvantage.

Achieve—Succeed with what you have to work with, but don't fault yourself for what you can't achieve because of lack of ability and resources.

Acid—If somebody talks with an acid tongue, remember his or her source is the hot air balloon between his or her ears.

Acid Rain—I hope all countries work together to rid the earth of acid rain, so we can save nature for all of mankind to enjoy.

Acid Rock—Thank God this music is gone.

Acknowledge—Express thanks for the talents of others, for it is through the recognition of others that we gain strength, not envy.

Acne—There is more to you than your face, so don't let this defeat you. Positive thinking shows on your face and lets the beauty from within shine through.

Acorn—Nice to see because it means you are in the heart of the country.

Acoustics—Some people have the wrong acoustics in their heads. They just hear sour note after sour note, while other people hear the sweet sound of life.

Acquaint—Get to know the nice things and people around you and be thankful for them.

Acquire—Get an education the best way you know and use it whenever possible.

Acquit—Free yourself from the guilt of your past by going on with your future.

Acre—Some people need a lot of land to spread their wings, and some people just need a little. No matter how much or how little land you have, just be thankful that you can spread your wings.

Acrobat—We are all walking on the tightrope of life. If you fall, just get back on it again. It isn't how many times you fall in life that counts; it's that you get back up each time.

Across—If you are having trouble getting to the other side, remember to take it slow, and you will make it.

Across-the-board—Don't let an across-the-board pay decrease get you down. Work for a brighter future for yourself and try hard enough, and before you know it you'll be chairman of the board.

Act—When you have the strength to help people in need, do it. If you can't he, say prayers for them so the help they need will come their way.

Action—Action does speak louder than words, but only if some good is done. If the action could cause some harm then it would be better to utter some harmless words.

Activate—Activate your mind, body, and soul into an Oscar-winning performance.

Active—Keep on moving. It is the only way you will see the fulfillment of your goals.

Act of God—Something we don't understand but we will when we meet the master.

Actor, Actress—A person who gets paid large sums of money for doing what the rest of us do in life for little or nothing.

Actual—Be sure what you tell somebody is the truth. Lying can get to be a bad habit. Only lie when it is in the best interest of a person or thing.

Acupuncture—This would make an ideal gift for someone who wants to experience something new and exciting.

Acute—Don't let acute pain slow you down. Let your acute will power speed you up.

Adam and Eve—This would be a great title for a Broadway show. There are a few people alive today who could play the part of the snake.

Adamant—Stick to your guns when it comes to decisions from the heart.

Adapt—Don't let changes throw you. It is by adapting that we survive.

Addict—Be sure if you are hooked on something, it is a good thing, not drugs.

Addition—If the minuses add up to more than your pluses in life, it's time you did some serious thinking and took action to reverse this.

Address—Direct your energy to your problems, and they will be solvable.

Adequate—Make sure you have met your needs, then pass the leftovers to people who are in need of some.

Adhere—Stick to your ideas, even though you are the only one who believes in them. It is what you think of yourself as a human being that counts, not what others think.

Adhesive tape—For people who talk too much, this comes in handy.

Adieu—Don't say goodbye to somebody before your hello has had a chance to sink in.

Adios—For a company that doesn't know when to leave, get yourself a parrot. Teach it to say, "Polly wants some peace and quiet." Maybe the next time they say they are coming. Polly will pay off for you.

Adjoin—A marriage joins you, so don't let an affair part you.

Adjust—When changes are needed for you to stay on the right track in life, make them. You can't go wrong when you use the sound judgment you were given naturally.

Ad-lib—In situations that make you nervous, ad-lib. It doesn't matter if something is not in the script, as long as you are comfortable with the task at hand.

Administer—Help those in need. People in nursing homes who have nobody need your support. Maybe someday you will be helped in return.

Admiral—He or she should be kind to those who are under them. We are all born equal; they should remember that.

Admire—It's okay to have high regards for others, but save some for yourself.

Admission—Let matters of the heart, soul, and mind be the deciding factors for a person's admission into a club. A person's race, religion, or politics should not enter the pictures at all.

Admit—Confess your mistakes and take a different path, and you will find the true way to fulfill your dreams.

Admonish—To disapprove of someone's specific faults is okay, but never judge anyone. Only God can do that.

Adolescence—A difficult growing-up period. You have advice coming to you from all directions. Listen to what's in your heart and take one day at a time.

Adopt—Father a child or giving birth to a child doesn't make a person a parent. Lay claim to a child by giving love to a child.

Adore—Adore God always.

Adorn—Don't put too much decorations on yourself. Natural beauty is what counts.

Adrift—Don't let your mind drift too far from home base; it may be too hard to get on track again.

Adult—What we are supposed to be when we grow up, but it doesn't hurt to keep some of the child in us.

Adultery—Some people think the other side is greener, but they forget that side has to be watered too.

Advance—Move forward, but don't forget where you came from.

Advance person—This person is probably more qualified to be a politician or a dignitary than the person he or she is advancing for, the reason being he or she has a powerful sense of direction that leadership needs.

Advantage—No matter how many or how few benefits you have, use them to produce a good effect on others.

Advent—A time to prepare for what Christmas is all about: the birth of Jesus.

Adventure—Life is an adventure with you trying to be yourself to the best of your ability.

Adverse—If your breath has an adverse effect on people, you could get a job as a bouncer. That way you wouldn't need to use as much bodily force, just breathe on them.

Advertising—Advertising either spoils your appetite at suppertime, makes you want to hop into bed for a love session, smash the television set in for indecent exposure, and puts you to sleep, or makes you want to rise and shine and march like a son of a gun.

Advice—Don't give any out unless you have to. There is enough hot air floating around already.

Advocate—Make sure the support you give somebody or something will help others with their struggle through life.

Aerial—Let your ideas go high up in the air, then reach for them and you will obtain them.

Aerialist—An aerialist is an acrobat who flies through the air with the greatest of ease. Now if he could only get his mother-in-law to quit fooling around with the net below.

Aerial ladder—Support your hometown fire department. If everybody in the country would do this, every fire department in the country would have one of these.

Affair—This starts out with love between the two parties involved. But can finish with hate if the noncheating wife or husband finds out about it. In other words an ugly divorce.

Affect—Be sure that no matter whoever or whatever you have an influence on, your influence is good and the results will benefit many people.

Affection—Don't hide love for others, it may be the thing that helps them make it through life.

Affidavit—Never lie under oath otherwise jail might be the closest thing to home you see for a while.

Affirm—Don't be afraid to state the truth. It may be tough to speak out, but the words will come out of your mouth.

Afflict—Never causes pain or suffering to someone or something unless in self-defense.

Affluence—If you have abundance, spread it around a little bit. You will be surprised at the good you can do.

Afford—If you can afford to yield to someone else, go ahead, for there is more pleasure in giving than receiving.

Affront—Make sure if you encounter someone face to face, you are doing it for the right purpose and not for your selfish self.

Afghan—This comes in handy to cuddle up to on a cold winter night.

Afloat—If you find yourself free of trouble, grab somebody else to take along. Give them the joy of this sensation too.

Afraid—Put your trust in the Lord, and you don't have to fear anything.

Africa—The second largest continent, lying south of Europe between the Atlantic and Indian Oceans. It is so beautiful it can take your breath away.

African violet—A roomful of these is a beautiful sight, especially at night lit up by artificial light. They give off peaceful radiance.

After—If you come later, don't feel bad. Take advantage of somebody else getting the path ready for you.

Afterglow—Some people experience afterglow after sex, other people feel like they have been through a washing machine, some feel like swinging on a chandelier, and a few sleep through the whole thing.

After-hours—When some affairs of the heart become realities of the night.

Afterlife—A chance to see the loved ones who have gone before us.

Afternoon—Take a nap if you are tired.

Afterpains—A woman goes through a lot to have a baby but what a beautiful miracle to behold.

After-shave—Wear the right kind, and the young women, will want to pursue you; wear the wrong kind, and old maids with electric blankets will want to lie down beside you.

Aftershock—Your husband helps you with the housework.

Afterthought—Better than no thought at all.

Afterworld—If some couples argue in the afterworld as much as they did during their lifetime, the rest of us mortals should ask for a rain check.

Again—Do something over and over until you get it right. Patience makes perfect.

Against—Better to be for something than against it.

Age—In God's world it doesn't matter how old a person is, because His love for all of us is ageless.

Agency—An employment agency is a very important service. They help people gain their dignity again.

Agenda—Be sure your program includes being kind to humans, animals, nature, and yourself.

Agent—The middle person in contract talks, but when they're over Fort Knox it is too small to hold his or her percentage of the salary awarded to their client; and if their client is a baseball player, they can build their own Fort Knox.

Agent Orange—This did more harm than good in the Vietnam War.

Age of Consent—The age at which a person is legally considered competent to give consent, as to sexual intercourse. I say sexual intercourse should be saved for marriage.

Age of reason—An age at which a person is considered capable of making reasoned judgments. You can't go by this because some people mature more quickly than other people.

Aggie—A wonderful and safe game for people of all ages to play.

Aggressive—Be bold and active when it comes to spreading good in the world. What a great world this would be if only more people would do this.

Aghast—A normal reaction to your annual property taxes.

Agile—An agile mind comes in handy when you witness a crime.

Agony—Don't let this get the best of you. You are in good company; Jesus Christ went through this too.

Agree—Try to be in accord with someone else, then march through life with this person. Two in step are sometimes better than one. Let that someone else be Christ.

Agriculture—Save it. Family farms run America. We can't afford to lose them.

Aground—Don't let running around stop you. There is only one way to go but up.

Ahead—Make sure that when you advance towards the future, your cause is acceptable to others, too. There is no greater personal happiness than making the world a better place to live for your fellowmen, too.

Aggie—A wonderful and safe a better place to live for your fellowmen, too.

Aid—Help those in need, because without help some people will always stay down and lose their human dignity.

Aide—A nurse aide is the best in the hospital. She or he has more contact with the patient than the doctor. They can change the mood of a patient from sad to happy so don't downplay their importance in a hospital.

AIDS—Don't allow it to kill the promise of tomorrow.

Ail—Pray for recovery, then watch God's plan work for you.

Aim—Try to hit the right career for yourself, and you will go a long way. Don't give up if you miss. Try again and again until you hit the bull's-eye.

Air—God's gift to breathers. Help keep it clean.

Airbag—A talkative person.

Air conditioning—Some people get so hot under the collar, even air conditioning can't cool them off.

Aircraft Carrier—Both men and women should be able to serve on this. Women are just as capable as men to do the work on the carrier. As far as sexual harassment goes, both men and women should have outgrown this by now. If not, they belong in Kindergarten and some of them might be outperformed by some of the children.

Airedale—This dog stands and walks in a dignified way.

Airfare—Sometimes this is so high, maybe it would be cheaper to flap your own arms and take off.

Air Force—The skies really are safer and friendlier with them looking after us.

Airhead—A person who doesn't listen to what is said to him or her. It goes through one ear and out of the other.

Airplane—Soar as high as you can with your ideas. After you reach your goal, pave the way for a smooth landing.

Air pocket—Constipation becomes a reality when a person is using the bathroom on an airplane and it hits an air pocket.

Airport—There is triple danger here everyday. In the airport they have to look out for people wanting to carry guns, bombs, and drugs aboard and many other things. On the airfield they have to look out for planes colliding while taking off and landing. In the air they have to look out for planes being on a collision course, terrorists being on the plane, drunk and rude passengers, bad weather, and crash landings. But don't be afraid to fly. There are trained personnel to look after you. Just put your trust in the Lord and take off.

Air Raid—One would hope this is obsolete forever.

Air rifle—Parents should supervise their kids, if the kids own one of these. The age of the kids can be a factor but one can never be too careful. Damage to buildings or injury to an innocent victim is nothing to sneeze at.

Airsickness—If this happens to you too many times, better to take something for it than the decoration you leave for the airline personnel to clean up.

Aisle—Some wedding parties are so large they should use their local interstate as the aisle to march down on.

Aladdin—Don't you wish you could have been him and asked for peace in the world.

Alamo—Scene of a siege and massacre of Texans by Mexican troops. The Texans had nothing to be ashamed of. We should remember them with pride and respect.

Alarm—Give a warning if it will prevent somebody from encountering danger.

Air raid—One would hope this is obsolete forever.

Air rifle—Parents should supervise their kids, if the kids own one of these. The age of the kids can be a factor but one can never be too careful. Damage to buildings or injury to an innocent victim is nothing to sneeze at.

Alarm clock—Don't curse it. Be thankful you can get out of bed and go to work. Some people can't.

Albatross—Don't let this be a constant, worrisome burden around your neck. Replace it with hope and success will be yours.

Albino—If you see an animal that is albino, consider yourself lucky. Treasure it because it doesn't happen too often that you see one of these.

Album—Take care of this because pictures of loved ones gone is a treasure to behold.

Alcohol—A little bit never hurt some people. Just learn to control it. Don't drive drunk. Drink at home and you can flop into bed if you drink too much.

Alert—Watch out for Satan. Sin is his game. Don't play it. It may be hard not to, but the reward will be great later on.

Algebra—This is fun to learn. Some students find it hard to learn. After you get the hang of it, it's a great tool to have.

Alibi—Don't make excuses for your mistakes. Take account of them and learn from them.

Alien—A creature from outer space. Some people act this way and dress this way on earth without realizing it. If you see one of them, don't make fun of him or her. Try to make the person realize the potential they have as a human being. The more people accept them, the less their difference will be noticed. They are just as human as the next person. They just have to realize it and they will become first class citizens.

Alienate—Don't alienate a friend because one friend lost means more friends lost.

Align—Be sure you keep your car in good condition. Remember to align the wheels of your car regularly.

Alike—Some people and twins are alike in some ways but everybody is different in his or her own way.

Alimony—Good to have for those who need it in order to survive.

Alive—Live your life to its fullest.

All—We are all in life together, so let's all work for peace together.

All-American—An American who treats everybody as equal and is kind and good to humans, animals, nature, and anything else under the sun.

All-Around—Some people are able to do many things well. If you can't don't fret, just be thankful for what you can do.

All Clear—A signal, usually by siren, that a danger has passed. If you hear this, don't forget to thank the people who watched for the danger to pass and set the all clear signal on.

Allege—Don't assert anything without or before proof because if you are wrong it may be too hard to recall your mistake later on.

Allegiance—Be loyal to your own true love.

Allergy—Don't let a sneeze get the best of you, especially if you wear a toupee.

Alleviate—Lessen the pain of others whenever possible. Simon and Veronica helped Jesus on His way to the cross. Help others so that their crosses won't be so painful.

Alley—Don't go up an alley unless you know what awaits you, especially at night.

Alley cat—Don't let the streets and alleys of America be overcrowded with unwanted cats and dogs: neuter and spay your pets.

Alliance—Form a union with other people to work for a more peaceful world.

Alligator—There are alligator bags, shoes, etc. Why can't we let the alligator be the alligator they were born to be?

All important—We are all important because by God, we are all born equal.

All-night—Don't go to all night parties because you will look like hell in the morning. You need your rest to look like heaven in the morning.

Allocate—Allot some time to your children everyday. America's future depends on your children.

Allow—Even if you are busy. Don't forget to allow yourself some time to think about God, your life and your future.

Allowance—Teach your children the value of money. Give them an allowance and tell them they have to budget it out for the week. Adult ways taught now will result in adult ways lived later.

All-purpose—Be useful in many ways. You never can tell when it will come in handy. In other words, be a jack of all trades and master of none.

All right—Be thankful if you feel all right because that means one less trip to your doctor.

All Saints' Day—November 1, the day on which a Christian feast honoring all the saints is observed. They did God's will even though it might have been a heavy cross to bear.

Allure—Don't charm too many women because one bride is enough for a lifetime.

Ally—Join with God and you will have a steady ally as you travel through life.

Almanac—A wonderful publication for you if you travel and also if you want information, usually statistical, on many subjects.

Almighty—Praise the Lord. He is omniscient, omnipotent and omnipresent.

Almond—Wonderful to use when you bake cakes or cookies.

Almost—To almost finish a race is nothing to be ashamed of. Maybe it was to the best of your ability. So hold your head up high and be proud of yourself.

Alms—Give money and goods to the poor and you won't live to regret it.

Aloft—Birds like to sit in high places and fly overhead and drop their greetings down below.

Aloha—A beautiful greeting from a beautiful state.

Alone—You don't have to feel this, because He that is in you is greater than what is outside the world and is always with you.

Along—Enjoy some independence; don't go along with everything people say or do.

Aloof—Don't be aloof when being friends with somebody would suit your style much better.

Aloud—Cry aloud for help but only if it will save your life or of any other.

Alphabet—A wonderful achievement for a young child to learn the alphabet.

Also-ran—There are no losers in a race. Everybody tries, so why care what position you wind up in? To try is the heart of the race, not the position of the finish.

Altar Boy—Don't take an altar boy for granted. You may be looking at the next pope.

Alternate—Always have one, two or more choices ready to use, if at first you don't succeed in life.

Aluminum—You think you have it bad, some people collect cans for a living.

Alumni—How come when homecoming is going on, the schools want the former students to come back to visit. When some of them were students, their teachers could have kicked their buttocks from here to China.

Always—At all times, remember your roots. They provide the foundation you can depend on for moral support.

Alzheimer's disease—Hats off to these brave souls. When you lose your memory, you lose memories that have been built up over the years. One would hope that they see the light pretty soon and that the cure for this dreadful disease is just around the corner.

Amass—If you amass a fortune, give some to the needy.

Amateur—They may not get paid like professionals, and maybe aren't quite as talented, but the joy they bring to the hearts, minds, and souls of people more than makes up for it.

Ambassador—Be God's representative in life. Help people find God, and you will share their joy in this new discovery.

Ambition—Don't hide this. Bring it forth and your success won't be far behind.

Ambulance—The people who work on an ambulance are brave because they never know what awaits them.

Ambulance chaser—This person should be ashamed of himself or herself. When you are in an accident, you are not in a condition to make a decision about suing somebody.

Ambush—Don't let Satan side track you on your way to heaven.

Amen—Amen for a short sermon on a Sunday when it is about 110 in the shade in a church with no air conditioning.

Amend—Change your lifestyle and remove yourself if you are on a crooked and narrow path. Step to the music of a straight and wide path and achieve your goals in life.

American Buauty—A beautiful rose but some women in America should be called this too. I am not talking about beauty on the outside. I am talking about the help they give to the poor and homeless. What is more beautiful than that.

American cheese—Thank Wisconsin for this and all the other dairy products they produce.

American dream—Having an equal chance to achieve your goals in life like anybody else.

American eagle—A beautiful sight in the air. A sickening sight lying on the ground shot by a human being just for the hell of it.

American Indian—They were here first, so why not treat them like it?

American nightmare—Your mother-in-law holds a black belt in Karate.

Americans—They make America what it is today: a great nation.

Amicable—A hello from a cheerful person can change the day for a depressed person. So don't be afraid to give those hellos out. You never know whose life you're changing.

Amish—Their perception of life is shown through the beauty of their quilts.

Amity—Let's pray for this everyday. When there are friendly and peaceful relations between nations, all God's children can enjoy peace.

Ammunition—You have the ammunition to get ahead in life: your brain. Use it. You'll be surprised at what comes forth.

Amnesia—Some people you would love to forget; other people make a memory worth while.

Amnesty—I hope all governments learn to grant pardon to people who, in their hearts, are working for a just cause.

Among—Surround yourself with good people, and maybe as a group you can change and world for the better.

Amorous—It's okay to be in love as long as it doesn't interfere with your job. Don't become a skirt-chasing, bun-pinching, flirting fool at your job.

Amount—See how much love you can spread through the world. Not sexual love but the good and kindness from your heart.

Amphitheater—A good place to hear an orchestra play. Also a good place to bring your children for fun and entertainment.

Ample—Don't worry if you are a large size. There are plenty of people in the same situation.

Amplify—Raise your voice for the needy and homeless. One more voice heard means more people helped.

Amputee—They achieve more in life than most people who have all their limbs.

Amsterdam—The constitutional capital and largest city of the Netherlands. The land of tulips, wooden shoes and wind mills. What a magic Kingdom to behold.

Amuse—If you are able to entertain people, don't be afraid to do it. The joy you provide them may be the only happiness they have in their lives.

Amusement Park—If tension runs too high at home sometimes with your family, take them to an amusement park to cool off.

Anaheim—Anaheim and Disneyland go together like a horse and buggy. They have brought joy to millions.

Ancestor—It doesn't matter where you came from as long as you know where you're going.

Anchor—Don't let anybody or anything hold you down. Build up your strength and overcome it.

Anchorage—It was founded in 1915 as construction headquarters for the Alaska Railroad. It is the largest city in Alaska. What a beautiful state Alaska is.

Anchorperson—A good one will keep you alert and informed about the news. A bad one will bore you and put you to sleep. One good thing is, if you don't like the person or persons you can change the channel or turn the television off.

Anchor store—If you are building a mall be sure you pick a good anchor store. The anchor store attracts customers who are then expected to patronize the other shops in the mall. A bad anchor store could close the whole mall down.

Ancient—Something ancient, but look how sturdy it is compared to some of the things made today.

Ancient History—A label given to persons or events that lose their importance in life, but it doesn't preclude a comeback by anybody or anything.

Anecdote—Tell an anecdote if it will cheer somebody up.

Anemia—If somebody you know has this, be supportive and say some prayers for him or her.

Angel—A good, steady companion to have around. Whether you believe in guardian angels or not is besides the point. Why knock it if it is comforting to someone you know and love for them to believe they have a special helper for life.

Angelfish—The name applies to a fish that cheers you up, and it does.

Angel food cake—A nice light cake to lighten you up.

Angle—Use the right angle, and you will come up with the right catch.

Angleworm—Some boys are afraid to handle one of these and use it as bait in fishing. If you are a boy and this follows you to manhood, don't let it bother you. There are many characteristics to judge a man and the least of them is handling an angleworm.

Angry—Don't waste your time being angry. Your time would be better spent spreading happiness around the world.

Anguish—Help those in pain. Remember it could be you in their place, so don't be afraid to help.

Animal cracker—A special treat for little kids and big ones too.

Animals—Be kind to them. They conquer loneliness by their presence to humans and they bring happiness to humans by their presence. Some people say when a certain person is bad, he or she acts just like an animal. That isn't so. The majority of animals don't act like bad humans. So don't compare bad humans to animals.

Animate—Bring life where there is darkness, and you will make the world a better place for all.

Animated Cartoon—A lot of work goes into this to make it so enjoyable when you see it. So appreciate the labor of love that goes into making this for the enjoyment of all.

Annex—Annex your mind, body, soul, and heart together for the right cause, and you can climb any mountain life has to offer.

Anniversary—Every year is special in a marriage. The importance being: every year is a building block towards a solid marriage. So treat every year of your marriage as an anniversary year. Special in its own way until death do you part. The memory of those years will be with you and your spouse for all eternity.

Announcer—A good one doesn't put you to sleep. He or she keeps you aware of what's going on in the world.

Annoy—Don't bother anybody. Look into a mirror instead and pester that image until it produces that results you need to improve your life.

Annual—Recheck your life every year and see how you are coming along. Are you making progress towards a more productive life?

Annul—If you annul your marriage don't rush off and make the same mistake twice.

Anorexia nervosa—One would hope that teenage women suffering from this get help. One good role model for them would be any woman who suffered from this and overcame it. Let's hope that two groups meet up and let the healing begin. Prayer also helps.

Another—An another one of you is probably what the world needs, especially if you are a good person.

Answer—The solution to your problems might be how hard you are praying for your requests. It also takes hard work and persistence on your part to get the job done.

Answering machine—Some of these are pleasant to listen to, some are annoying, some put you to sleep, some are boring and some are downright nasty.

Answering service—This is okay as long as the person on the other side is friendly. If the person is not friendly, better off with no service at all.

Ant—Ants may be small but look at what they can do acting as a unit. The same goes for people.

Antelope—A beautiful animal to see running in the wild and enjoying nature as God intended it to be.

Antenna—The way some people act you would think their antennae need adjusting.

Anthem—May your anthem be the song that brings the most joy to your heart.

Anti-American—People who don't know America and Americans very well. If they did, they wouldn't be anti-American anymore. The freedom in America and the nice people can't be surpassed by any country.

Antichrist—An enemy of Christ. How can anybody be an enemy of a man who died on the cross for everybody.

Anticipate—Take life one day at a time. You will find it easier to cope with it that way.

Anticlimactic—If something is anticlimactic, maybe the next time you plan an event, you should save your excitement for the event itself and not for the planning of it.

Antipathy—You may have a strong dislike for someone, but that isn't their problem; it's yours.

Antiperspirant—Some people don't believe in using this. Of course some people can't help the wet under their arms. Those people who can help it, should be called, "twin lakes."

Antique—Any material thing that is really old is considered valuable. Why don't we treat people the same way? As they get older, we should seek out their wisdom instead of shutting them off from society.

Antisocial—Don't be this way. Otherwise if you become hostile to or disruptive of the established social order, you might end up in the slammer.

Anxiety—Don't let it rule over you, otherwise it can ruin your life. Get professional help if needed.

Anywhere—Love has the possibility of being anywhere. If it isn't where you are, start it and watch it spread.

Apart—When you are away from someone you care for, you will realize how important she or he is in your life. So when you see them again, show your appreciation for them.

Apartment—Do your part to keep the apartment building you live in a first-rate dwelling for all.

Apathy—Politics can do this to you, especially on the national scene, but never let it happen to you locally. Your local government is your heart and soul, so be a part of it or work for change.

Apocalypse—The end of the world is nothing to be afraid of. Live right and you will do okay on judgment day.

Apology—An apology from the heart is the only thing that counts.

Apostle—I think we are all on a special mission for Christ. When you see a poor person, see Christ in him or her and help them. You then, will have achieved your true purpose in life.

Apostles' Creed—A beautiful statement of belief. Say it when you begin doubting yourself as a human being created in the image and likeness of God.

Appalling—The living conditions of the homeless.

Apparel—If you have enough clothes, share some with those people who don't.

Appeal—Any turtle in the land moves faster than the appeals process of our court system in this country.

Appear—Look happy and it will spread to others.

Appearance—May your appearance be pleasing to the eye, because already there is too much eye strain in this world.

Appease—Let's hope someday that somebody comes forward to bring peace to the entire world.

Appetite—Keep your appetite under control, or you will be the big top performer in the elephant line.

Applause—Show praise when someone deserves it, especially your children.

Apple—They claim an apple a day keeps the doctor away. I don't believe it because the doctors keep coming, or should I say we have to keep going to the doctor. Doctor's don't make house calls. Most of them don't, anyway.

Appliance—Use the appliance known as the mind as much as possible and the waste material in your head will be limited.

Application—Use the skills given to you, and you will help make a better world for all.

Appoint—Appoint yourself as a good will ambassador. Choose some deputies and spread goodwill around the world.

Appointment—Don't you hate it when you have to wait in your doctor's office waiting room to pass your appointed time. Then they have you go to another room and you have to wait some more. They also have you disrobed and have you covered up with a small sheet that barely covers your body. It is also cold in the room. The doctor finally comes and keeps his or her hand on the doorknob. In other words they can't get out of the room fast enough, leaving you with a ton of questions.

Appraise—Appraise your lifestyle and see if your career goals are being met. If not, tune-up your energy and focus yourself on the goals that will advance your career and give you a good feeling about yourself.

Appreciate—Think well of everybody, and it will be returned to you in a greater amount.

Apprehend—Apprehend what you can, and what you can't—the hell with it—life goes on.

Apprentice—Learn your trade well, and you will help America build its future.

Approach—Parents should tell their children not to approach strangers and be careful if strangers approach them. Otherwise their children might become a stranger to them for a period of time they won't forget.

Appropriate—It's appropriate to begin a relationship when you have a peace of mind about it, all systems are going, and you feel it's the right thing to do.

Approval—Just because you don't approve of somebody doesn't mean their lifestyle is wrong.

April—What a beautiful dream to have, to be in Paris with an umbrella in one hand and a sense of adventure in the other.

April Fool's Day—If you play a joke on somebody, be sure you are willing to have one played on you. The sooner you learn life is a two-way street, the quicker you can travel it.

Apron Strings—It's not so bad to be tied to your mother's or wife's apron strings. It's better than being tied to your mother-in-law's or someone else's wife's apron strings.

Aptitude—No matter how quick or slow you learn, learn according to the speed you are comfortable with.

Aptitude test—Don't feel bad if your child scores low on this, because sometimes hidden talents don't show up in the test results.

Aquarium—If you have an aquarium, take care of it and watch the fish enjoy themselves. Compared to the fish who have to swim in the pollution of some of the lakes and streams of today, your fish are lucky.

Arabia—Let's hope the people of Arabia and Israel can live in peace forever.

Arbitrator—Let's hope they are fair with everybody once their decision is made

Arbor Day—Plant a tree and take care of it. Make America more beautiful, if that's possible.

Arch—Do your part to build an arch for peace and let it stand forever.

Architecture—Buildings should be designed for the comfort of the people inside, not for how it looks to people passing by the outside.

Archives—If the walls of rooms in some business places could talk, maybe you would have a steamy novel on your hands.

Arctic—A beautiful region. It may be cold, but it shows God's creation in an unspoiled state. So don't complain about cold states or countries. Anybody who can survive a cold region is a true, warm human being at heart. The warmth of which you can't compare with anything.

Area—Let your area of expertise be the area you are most comfortable with, not the one that society wants you to be in.

Argentina—Argentina makes me think of the tango. So go out and learn it and get a workout.

Argue—Don't argue when love is so much better.

Aristocrat—Everybody is upper class in God's eyes.

Arithmetic—Make sure your pluses outweigh your minuses in life, and you will do all right.

Ark—Some people drive a Cadillac, but Noah got by with an ark. It isn't the style you drive in life that counts, it's how you maneuver with what you have.

Arlington National Cemetery—A peaceful setting for the brave of this country. They fought the wars for the freedom we enjoy now. So hang on tight to it, because you will never know a more precious gift.

Arm—Years ago it took an arm and a leg to pay for something. Now it takes the whole body.

Armadillo—Give one to somebody who is hard to buy for.

Armed Forces—They protect us so that we can live in peace.

Armful—Take your children in your arms and say, "I love you."

Armistice Day—Let's hope this day is remembered and no more wars are fought.

Armor—Too much starch in your washing machine, and your clothes will fit like this. Don't fret, just keep a stiff upper lip.

Army—Bless them, for they are defending our freedom.

Aroma—Use the right deodorant and people won't be able to smell you a mile away.

Around-the-clock—Some people work around-the-clock while other people lay around-the-clock and I don't mean people who are bedridden.

Arraign—Don't miss your arraignment even if you are innocent, otherwise jail might be your sweet home for a while.

Arrange—Arrange your life so all your time is precious and not wasted.

Arrangement—An arranged marriage is not so bad if you get to see your intended spouse beforehand, but you may be a victim of cardiac arrest if you don't.

Arrears—It's time to quit charging when you become guilty of this.

Arrest—It seems when a crime is committed nowadays, the victim feels more like the arrested party than the perpetrator does.

Arrive—If you arrive late for dinner parties and other events, maybe you'll be sitting home more. People don't like to see their guests coming late to their dinner parties or events. So your name may disappear from their invitation list.

Arrogance—Some people are so arrogant they could give a 747 competition.

Arrow—Be careful of love that is not straight from the heart and feels more like an arrow up the behind. That is the kind you can do without.

Arsenic—Sometimes this is used to kill a human being. How horrible! Let's hope the guilty are caught and sent to prison for life.

Arson—Some people do this to collect insurance money. What a dirty shame when you think of some people who really need it and have an honest reason to collect it and are denied it.

Art—Enjoy it and support it. It is a joy to behold.

Artery—May your main road lead you to happiness.

Arthritis—Get this and you will know what pain is all about.

Article—Learn to be a good journalist and maybe there wouldn't be so many newspapers under the bottom of birdcages.

Artificial—Be natural at all times. People will realize what they see in you is what you really are.

Ascend—Go up to your highest goal, then work for being better at it everyday.

Ascension Day—Jesus may have ascended into heaven, but he left us the perfect example to live by: Himself.

Ash—Out of the ashes will come the rose, so don't let your problems overcome you, because they can be conquered.

Ashamed—There are times you are going to feel humiliated or embarrassed, but don't let that overcome you.

Ash Wednesday—The symbol of the state we will return to, but it is not permanent because our resurrection is assured by the death and resurrection of Jesus.

Ask—Don't be afraid to seek information. If you learn enough, someday you will be the giver instead of the seeker.

Asleep—Did you ever hear the joke about the preacher who gave a sermon so boring that he fell asleep while giving it?

Aspire—Aspire to be yourself and do your best.

Ass—Maybe it isn't nice to say but the way some people act, they remind me of this.

Assassin—They destroy the God-given right to live. Also, another name for a coward because most of the time they don't face their victims. The victims aren't given a chance to defend themselves.

Assault—If you are a victim of this, defend yourself; it's a matter of life or death.

Assembly Line—The heart of America, because without them there would be no pride in America.

Assert—Express yourself more forcefully or boldly if your shyness is beginning to control your life.

Assessor—Don't blame this person for increased taxes on improvements to your house, because beauty is in the eyes of the beholder.

Asset—Be an asset to peace, and you will help it to be the world's top priority.

Asshole—Some people measure up to this.

Assignment—Work on the assignment of being yourself the best. It is the greatest assignment you will have in your life.

Assistant—If you think assistants aren't important, just look at the President of the United States. He or she couldn't make it through the day without their help. So when you get right down to it, who do you think has the real power in Washington, D.C.

Associate—Associate with the good things in life and help them spread.

Assortment—It takes an assortment of people to make the world, so don't leave anybody out when you say everybody is born equal.

Assume—Don't take anybody or anything for granted, for when they are gone, you realize what you miss.

Assure—Give confidence to someone in need of it. Make sure, though, you leave a little bit for them to develop themselves. For it is only through doing for self that we become self.

Asterisk—God has an asterisk by everybody's name with reference to a footnote. The footnote being, "Everybody is born equal." Being born equal to everyone means being just as important as the President of the United States and movie stars.

Asthma—The sudden recurring attacks of labored breathing, chest constriction, and coughing are the characteristics of this disease. One hopes anybody who has this doesn't give up. For when we give up, we give up hope. With hope you can overcome this, so don't give up.

Astonish—Surprise someone who needs some excitement in his or her life.

Astray—If you think the right path is too beaten up, instead of straying away from it, start a new one.

Astrology—It doesn't hurt to study the stars, just so you aren't so dazed by them that you forget to look where you are going on earth.

Astronaut—They are shot off into space and do an important job for our country. The way some people act on earth, the astronauts could get the same effects as they do in space, if they could get inside these people's heads.

Atheists—They believe in something, because they believe in the idea of no God.

Athletes—The highest paid athletes are not the best athletes. The best athletes are the lowest paid ones who have hearts of gold.

Atlas—Don't take the problems of the world on your shoulders, if you can't even handle your own problems.

Atmosphere—Make the surroundings around you cheerful and people will enjoy them and you more.

Atom Bomb—See one and that's one too many. It's an abomination. Let's hope it never becomes a reality in life again.

Atone—Atone for your sins, but then get on with your life.

Attachment—Attachment to somebody or something is okay as long as you leave room for yourself to live an independent life.

Attack—Never attack anybody or anything unless in self-defense.

Attain—No matter how much wealth you attain, you still can't take it with you. Somebody will someday figure out a way to take it. So don't be surprised if someday you see a moving van behind a funeral procession.

Attempt—Attempt to do the best you can everyday, because it's to your advantage to be at your best in the competitive world of today.

Attendance—Don't judge a person by the size of his or her funeral. Some of the world's biggest heels have big funerals, and some of the people with the gentlest of hearts have small ones.

Attendant—If this person works in a high-class restroom. You can be sure he or she could get enough material for a steamy novel.

Attention—Pay attention to your eyes, for they are the windows of your world. You can't control what goes by you, but you can control how you react to it. So take care of your eyes so that you can always have a clear vision of the world before you and you can react properly to the situation at hand.

Attention Deficit Disorder—A child who has this should be given the benefit of the doubt and the best professional help he or she can get. To be treated as normal as possible as a child should be the goal of the parents for the child.

Attest—What you attest to in court to be true, make sure it is. Otherwise it will be affirmed you are going to jail in an official capacity.

Arctic—Rediscover the treasure chest of your past. Go through your attic, which could hold the keys to your future. It is only when you appreciate the past that you can realize the potential of your future.

Attire—Don't try and keep up to the next person when it comes to clothes. Spend according to your means and you will be better off financially. Also, you will look like a million dollars whether you believe it or not. You don't have to spend the most to look the best.

Attitude—Let your attitude be a positive one so that today's happiness can be shared with others for a better tomorrow for all concerned.

Attorney General—Elect a good one in your state, and instead of a giant, crime will seem more like an ant in your state.

Attraction—Don't get attracted to the wrong person, otherwise you might get hooked up to a horse of a different color. In other words, instead of a Shetland pony on your hands, you'll have a bronco.

Auctioneer—They are faster than a speeding bullet, louder than your mother-in-law, and a good one can sell the shirt off your back right on the spot.

Audience—Don't be afraid of people. They provide an opportunity to have your ideas heard.

Audit—Take account of yourself once a year. See if there is room for improvement, then set up your goals for the year.

Audition—Don't let an audition scare you. The more you do it, the more at ease you will become.

Auditor—They check the books and listen to the people pacing behind them. The carpet companies love them.

Auld Lang Syne—Remember the good old days and use your power to help recreate them.

Authentic—Everybody claims this but some people play games and then their origins are questioned.

Author—Everyone should write a book. Whether it gets published or not is beside the point. Once you get it out of your system, you feel good.

Authority—Respect the power some people have. Someday it may be yours too. Use it wisely and be kind to those below you.

Authorize—Authorize your heart to let the love flow.

Autobiography—Write your biography and see your life as you never have seen it before.

Autograph—Give yourself a boost: buy yourself an autograph book and sign your name in it everyday.

Automated Teller Machine—Used when you want cash in a hurry, but it is spent faster than you obtain it.

Automatic Pilot—A mind set too long on automatic pilot loses its power to think for itself. So keep your mind active, and you will be able to manage a variety of options in your life.

Automation—I don't mind progress as long as the robots are friendly and can strike up a good conversation.

Autopsy—Don't judge a person's character by the results of this because the true circumstances of a person's life aren't revealed in an autopsy.

Autoworker—If management would show them the respect they deserve, then they would produce the cars we deserve. Also, foreign car sales would go down.

Autumn—Proof that there is a God. Look at all the beautiful colors.

Auxiliary—They help people in need to become people without need.

Avail—Avail yourself where charity is concerned.

Avalanche—An avalanche of love is needed in this world more than ever.

Average—Nobody is average. God made a masterpiece out of everyone. Some people don't use their abilities the right way.

Avoid—Keep away from bad habits, or else you may become a bad habit that people will avoid.

Awake—Be sure you are awake when you drive.

Award—It seems every time you turn around there is another awards show. When are they going to give an award to God's chosen people, like those who work in a nursing home or drive an ambulance?

Aware—Know your surroundings, and you will know the direction you want to take in your journey through life.

Away—Don't stay away from home too long. The people keeping the home fires burning may just put them out.

Awe—Treat yourself once in a while and look in a mirror and discover the magic you possess.

Awkward—A man giving a speech unaware that his fly is open.

Axe—If you have an axe to grind, be careful you don't grind it so long as you lose the direction of your life.

Axis—May your axis in life rotate in the direction that will get the best results for you.

Babbler—If you know a person who is one of these, you know what hot air is all about.

Baboon—Nice to see at the zoo but not as a house pet. What a mess! Mr. Clean would grow hair on his head before he got done cleaning up.

Baby—A beautiful gift of God. Take care and love her or him, and you will see the wonderment of this miracle grow before your eyes.

Baby Boomer—A member of a baby-boom generation. One hopes social security will be around for them when they retire. They worked hard and have earned it.

Baby Grand—Beautiful to have, but if you can't afford one, remember, you don't miss what you don't have. If you did own one, would you play it or would it be another thing in your house collecting dust.

Babysitter—Both the parents and the babysitter should know each other, because either one could be the victim of a stranger in a situation like this. The more we learned about each other, the more peace of mind each can obtain for the sake of the children.

Bachelor—A single man. He can water the grass, but he doesn't have to cut it.

Back—Take care of your back; it is your greatest support in life.

Backache—A bad one is what pain is all about.

Backbone—No matter how weak or strong your is, work with it.

Backbreaking—Trying to recreate your honeymoon on your twenty-fifth wedding anniversary by carrying your wife over the threshold. Especially if you are out of shape and she is overweight.

Back burner—What you put on the back burner may backfire on you. The item may belong to the front burner. Double check items you put on the back burner, otherwise it may be too late to recall them for the front burner.

Backdoor—Don't take the backdoor in you house for granted. It has more activity than the front door. The backdoor has the home sweet home feeling.

Backdrop—May your backdrop in life be the perfect setting for you to make it through life.

Background—Be sure your background is perfectly clean when you apply for the job you want perfectly clear.

Backlash—You handle backlash by admitting to your mistakes or holding firm to your true convictions. Nothing is gained by standing still.

Backlog—The backlog in government paperwork would make many fireplace owner in America happy.

Backpack—For fresh air, exercise and a healthier you, backpack. You never know what new discoveries you'll see in nature.

Backpedal—Don't backpedal so much on issues that people nickname you, "The Reversal Kid."

Backseat driver—If you have a passenger who is one of these, pull over to the side of the road and let him or her drive. Let him or her experience for himself or herself how crazy some people drive.

Backstage—If people could see what happens backstage at a theater, they would get more for their money while attending a play.

Backstretch—This is where you put your greatest effort to capture the homestretch.

Back talk—Years ago and I mean years ago, if a child did this, sometimes it meant washing the child's mouth out with soap and water. Now when a child does this, sometimes nothing is done. They could at least be sent to their room.

Backup—You know you have a good marriage when your spouse is there for you in times of trouble.

Backward—It's okay to go towards the rear for less pressure; just remember where the front is in case you ever feel like taking on the world again.

Backwoods—Go here when you need a place to think free of pressure.

Backyard—A great place for family gatherings.

Bacon—Even though you bring home the bacon, it wouldn't hurt you to take your turn at frying it once in a while, too.

Bad—The opposite of good, but it can be corrected if you work at it.

Bacteria—Make sure you wash your hands after going to the bathroom.

Bad Blood—Blood is a precious quality of life, so don't think the word bad to it and spoil life.

Badge—Not everyone has a badge to show off their contribution to life. Some people have invisible badges which are just as powerful as the visible ones.

Badlands—You don't have to go to Europe to see beauty. See America first, like the Badlands in South Dakota.

Badminton—Relax once in a while with a game of badminton.

Badmouth—Don't criticize anybody unless you can produce better results.

Bag—A cheaper method than plastic surgery, wear a bag over your head.

Baggage—Don't be afraid to ask for help if the luggage in your life gets too heavy. Some people are better carriers than others.

Baggy—Some teenagers wear such baggy trousers, you could put a house inside the trousers.

Bag lady—It's sad when you think that some of these women are smart enough to be carrying briefcases filled with business papers instead of shopping bags with all their possessions in them.

Bagpipe—Learn to play the bagpipe, and you will have accomplished something worthwhile in your life.

Bahamas—A beautiful place and a great vacation spot.

Bail—Set high enough, this can keep a person in jail. But how can you set it high enough if the crime is murder? Only one set of numbers apply to the victim—priceless—and how can you match that as far as punishment for the criminals goes?

Bailiff—Too bad the wonderful record they have of keeping order in the courtroom, couldn't be transferred outside onto the streets.

Bait and Switch—People who do this should be given the bend and kick. In other words, have them bend over and then give them a good kick in the behind.

Bake—Bake a cake for someone who needs a lift in their life.

Baker's Dozen—It would be nice to see this former custom among bakers come back. What the world needs now more than ever is good will shown towards people. Let one business like the bakery start it and I am sure other business places will follow.

Balance Beam—Life can be like a balance beam: a narrow and short path, so spread your wings (arms) to stay on top. If you fall, get back on and adjust your wing—spread to steady your balance. That is the important thing about life, when you fall, get up and go on with your life. Life was meant to be the victory after the fall, not the defeat from the fall.

Balcony—More of life can be seen from a balcony than from a front row seat, so don't feel bad if the action seems far away. You are closer to it than what you think.

Bald—Having no hair is nothing to be ashamed of. A few people have hair but don't have the brains to go with it.

Bald Eagle—Save the one symbol that means freedom for all.

Balky—A mule with a mind of its own and a kick to prove it.

Ballad—A good one brings you closer to the person or place it is about. Memories of home sweet home.

Balladeer—Sing a ballad that will turn a sorrowful heart into a happy one.

Ballerina—It takes blood, sweat, and tears to be one of these.

Ballgame—A game, especially baseball, that is played with a ball. Nice game to see and relax. Not so nice to see when the game turns into a brawl. The baseball players should be ashamed for the example they set for the kids and adults watching the game. One hopes the players quit the brawling and play the game in peace instead.

Balloon—They should make everybody happy as they float in the air, because they should remind us of America: freedom.

Ballot—If you run for office and the only vote you get is the one you cast for yourself, that's not so bad. It shows you believe in yourself. In order to achieve something in life, you have to start with belief in self.

Ballpark—One would hope all sports teams have a decent park or stadium to play in. If they don't, the city or the state they play in should figure out a way to build them a new one. Because if they leave, what a blow to the economy of the area they play in.

Ballroom Dancing—This form of dancing is in the same league as ma, apple pie, and baseball. Let's hope it stays popular, so we can see what people look like when they dance instead of wondering what spaceship they came off of.

Ballyhoo—Let's do this when all the homeless have a place of their own to call home.

Balmy—It may be mild and pleasant outside some days, but at the same time some people are trying to survive the eye of the storm inside of themselves. The weather doesn't mean the same to all people all the time.

Baloney—Better to remember this as a good tasting snack than slang for nonsense.

Baltimore Oriole—A beautiful bird and a good baseball player, too.

Ban—Don't ban anything that will increase the flow of love in life.

Banana—Eat plenty of them, because they are good for you.

Band—Let the music play on; just so long as it doesn't disturb the neighbors.

Bandage—What an invention this was! It helps to close wounds, stops the bleeding and helps to protect wounds from germs. A mother is relieved when she puts a bandage on her child's wound. For some wounds it is a miniature lifesaver. In hospitals it is a giant of a lifesaver. Anyway you put it, a bandage is good for life.

Bandit—Somebody who wants something for nothing, leaving society to pick up the tab every time.

Bandleader—A good one will let the band play, guiding the band's playing with his baton. A bad one will do the playing with his baton instead of the band.

Bandshell—Support the upkeep of the local bandshell in your community, because the music heard from it may be a major uplift for a lot of people in your community.

Bandwagon—It's all right to climb on the bandwagon, just make sure you know what tune is playing.

Bang—Be sure the bang you provide in life is friendly and not violent.

Bangs—Bangs for the hair make for a cute America.

Banish—When you get up each morning, banish all your doubts and fears of what lays ahead for you. Running at a level of one hundred percent confidence will assure you a first place in the performance of yourself for another day.

Banister—Relive your youth, slide down a banister.

Banjo—Anyone who can play it fast brings joy to people who want a faster pace to their life.

Bank—Make sure your spiritual account is just as full as your monetary account.

Bank Account—Spend money according to your bank balance; otherwise, overdraft charges will hold you ransom and take away the spending power in your life.

Bankcard—It used to be that money talks; now it's plastic that talks.

Banker—A good one knows where the buck stops.

Bankrupt—When you can't rob Peter to pay Paul anymore, because Peter started spending money like Paul.

Banner—Raise one once in a while and show where you stand in life.

Banquet—If you have a banquet, remember to invite some of the needy.

Baptism—When a child's world becomes God's world.

Baptism of fire—Hell to go through, but how much stronger you are after it's over.

Bar—Plan ahead if you like to drink. Call a taxi or bring a friend along who will stay sober and can drive you home.

Barbarian—People who act this way are lacking something. Otherwise they wouldn't act this way. They are lacking the love of God in their heart and soul.

Barbecue—A good way to fix food, and you get some fresh air at the same time.

Barbed wire—Don't close your mind like a barbed wire fence if you need help with a problem. It is only through openness with others that the survival of your tomorrow is possible.

Barber—The person to go to when you can't see where you're going anymore.

Bare—Some people shouldn't go bare because it's hard on the eyes.

Bareback—Don't ride a horse bareback if you aren't sure of yourself on a horse. A horse of a different color may show up and give you the ride of your life, and you'll need all the support you can get.

Barefoot—Years ago you could go barefoot through the park. Now if you go barefoot through the park, you have to be careful not to step on discarded hypodermic needles, dog you-know-what, and lovers making out in every which way.

Barf bag—Thank goodness the airlines have these on hand for passengers who have airsickness. If they didn't have them the cleaning crew would have their hands full.

Barfly—A person who frequents drinking establishments should not drink and drive. If they thought of the innocent victims driving past their cars, they wouldn't drink and drive. They would think of it if they hit one of the innocent victims what would happen. Death or injuries would occur. If this isn't a concern to them they have no heart. If this is the case, they should be sent to jail.

Bargain—Be good and when you die you go to heaven.

Bargain basement—Every store should be a bargain basement. Reduced prices on every floor means more customers on every floor. More customers means more money and the cash registers ringing to their heart's content.

Bargaining chip—If you don't have one in a negotiation, don't worry. If you use yourself to the best of your ability, that is your bargaining chip.

Barge—A barge may not be a fancy ship but it is worth its weight in gold for what it can do. Look at all the freight it transports. It is a gem of a boat.

Barhop—Poor people do it by walking, middle-income people do it by car, and rich people do it by jet.

Baritone—No matter what range you sing, singing in a choir or chorus is a good experience. It builds character. It makes a good person out of you.

Bark—A good sound if you are concerned about burglars entering your home.

Barker—A desperate used car salesman.

Barn—A symbol for the beautiful animals God created.

Barn dance—A good way to exercise.

Barnstorm—It's all right to barnstorm your way through life, just don't forget where your roots are.

Barnswallow—Not a pedigree of the bird world but a pedigree in God's world.

Barnyard—It may smell, but it doesn't have crime like the heart of the city.

Barracks—Home of the courageous and defenders of the red, white, and blue.

Barrel—A barrelful of laughs. Release some once in a while and make some people happy.

Barren—Don't let this stop you from enjoying life. Adopt a child and show your strength through the love you can provide for a child.

Barrier—No barrier can separate you from the power of your mind to survive any ordeal you are put through.

Barstool—These are built too high for the drinking people who fall off of them. What a hard fall!

Bartender—A very important job, because you must decide who has had too much to drink. Also, the best psychiatrist in the world.

You have to listen to everybody's problems, and you don't charge anything for it.

Base—Build a strong foundation and watch your career goals take off.

Baseball—The seventh inning stretch in baseball is the most exercise some people experience in a lifetime.

Basement—If your life seems like a basement, don't feel bad, because you are holding up the main floor for other people and you have strength beyond compare.

Bash—It's all right to have a party as long as a fight doesn't break out. For one guest to hit another guest with a heavy, crushing blow doesn't belong at a party or anyplace else. Also, for one person to criticize harshly, accusatorially, and threateningly another person doesn't help matters. I think when you have a party you should screen your guests. This way it will be a pleasant experience and not a regretful one.

Bashful—It's all right to be shy as long as you take responsibility for yourself as a human being.

Basic—The basic thing to surviving life is: live life, don't try to understand it.

Basketball—The losers of this game may not have the most points, but sometimes they have the most heart.

Basket case—A lawyer cross-examining a hostile witness who happens to be a national debate champion.

Basket weave—Don't be ashamed if this is your hobby. It is better than being stretched out on a floor from drug abuse.

Basset hound—A nice dog to come to after a hard day of work.

Bassoon—Not the daintiest instrument in the world, but it gives a giant message with the music it produces.

Bastard—A name given to a child born outside of wedlock. But who cares about the circumstances of the child's birth? It is still a creation of God to be loved and cared for. I will say, though some men are bastards, and it has nothing to do with the circumstances of their birth.

Bat—Why do some baseball players throw their bat in disgust when they strike out? It's not the bat's fault. The space between their ears calculated the situation wrong, so they should be kind to their bat.

Bats—I don't think bats the various nocturnal flying mammals, are anything to be afraid of. They don't harm humans. They just feed on insects, nectar, fruit, flesh, or blood. They don't feed on humans.

Batboy—Some will become the next baseball stars.

Batch—A batch of dough equals a batch of cookies, which equals a batch of fat if eaten all at once. So watch what goes in your mouth in a short period of time.

Bath—If people wear clothes pins on their noses around you, it's time for a bath.

Bathrobe—When you are sick or want to lounge around, this provides stiff competition to the family dog for man's best friend honors.

Bathroom—It means comfort when nature calls. But when nature calls while you are out in the nature, comfort may mean a big tree to hide oneself while you do your duty.

Bathtub—Be careful getting in and out of a bathtub. It's a hard place to take a fall. Also, don't set anything electrical near the tub while taking a bath. It's all right to be charged up when tackling a new day, but don't do it this way.

Baton—So what if a male twirls a baton in a band or marching unit. The object is to entertain. Society's stereotyping of who should do what in life should be put to rest once and for all.

Battered child—No human being should have to take this. One hopes help arrives for the battered children, women and even some men of the world.

Battering ram—Sometimes a few men have to use this in order to have sex with their wives. To avoid sex the wives have the bedroom door locked with furniture piled against the door.

Battle-ax—If you are married to one, your "I do" on your wedding day should have been "I don't" loud and clear.

Battle cry—Make sure your battle cry is to help all those in need within your means and grasp.

Bawl—If you hear this, help if you can or call for help if you can't help.

Bay of pigs—The invasion of Cuba ended in failure and a rout. The men who invaded Cuba were heroes even though they lost.

Bay window—What a pleasure to look out one of these to see nature at its best.

Bazaar—A good place to find a gift for that special someone in your life.

BB Gun—Not a good toy for children who don't know the harm it can cause somebody.

Be—Be good, be wonderful, and be what you want to be, because to be your natural self is to experience life on your terms not somebody else's.

Beach—Help keep the beach clean for everybody to enjoy.

Beacon—Every effort should be made to save the lighthouses of the world for the next generation to enjoy.

Bead—A rosary a day keeps the devil away.

Beagle—A cute dog to have as a pet, because it brings a smile to your face every time you see it.

Beam—Smile and you may start a habit that will be picked up by others.

Bean—If you have a secret you want kept, don't tell a babbler. They'll spill the beans every time, and you'll receive more coverage than The New York Times can give you.

Beanpole—People may consider you a bean pole, but when it comes to smarts, you may have a wide horizon to your credit.

Bear—Bear down on your problems, not the loved ones around you.

Beard—Nice to have on a cold day, and when certain undesirables come around, you can scare them off with the promise of a kiss and a bear hug. Most of all, wear it for your own sake.

Bear hug—Give to a person who you wish would drop out instead of dropping in at your house.

Bearskin rug—If it starts to move, you know it was pulling somebody's leg when it was shot.

Beat—Beat a rug, not a child.

Beautician—A good occupation because you are beautifying America. You need patience, though, but it is worth it. By giving a person a new hairdo, you are giving them an uplift they probably needed.

Beauty—The inner kind is more important, because it isn't just skin deep, it has substance.

Beauty spot—On a very talkative person it's his or her mouth, when it's shut.

Beaver—One who works harder than a lot of people on earth.

Bed—You heard the saying, "you made your bed; now lay in it." That's not so bad, just remember to straighten it out once in a while.

Bedmate—Make sure the person with whom you share a bed with is your wife or husband. Live according to our lord's rules and you will gain a ticket to heaven after you die.

Bed of roses—If your life is like a bed of roses, snip a dozen off and send it to a person whose life is like a bed of thorns.

Bedpan—Not the most beloved pan in the world, but it gives Rolaids and Tums competition for spelling relief.

Bedridden—Don't let being confined to a bed mean the same thing for your mind. Sometimes the mind has to do double duty, so allow it to do its job.

Bedroom—Some couples experience more exercise in this room than in their local gym.

Bedside manner—Change doctors if this becomes a bigger problem to you than what ails you.

Bed wetting—Don't let this overcome you. You can defeat it and go on with your life. A lot of people have overcome this. You just don't hear about it because of the shame connected with it. You don't have to feel this way because with your victory over this, you gain the freedom to talk about it. Who knows, maybe someday you may want to help somebody else going through the same thing you did.

Bee—It isn't so bad to have a bee in one's bonnet, just so your bee is in your bonnet and not somebody else's.

Beefcake—Don't feel bad if you don't have the body to be a Chippendale dancer or a model. If you can get out of bed in the morning, what more can you ask for?

Beehive—Years ago it was a hairstyle; now the bees have reclaimed their turf.

Beeline—Make a beeline for home after work if you want to drink. Better to take a few snorts at home than to zigzag down the highway after a few at a bar.

Before—Before your time is up on earth, get to know God because he is a good fellow to come home to.

Beggar—Be careful you don't charge too much, for tomorrow you might be this.

Beginner—Give a beginner just learning something new, a chance in life, because the future of America depends on it.

Begrudge—Don't waste time on begrudging, because your development as a first-rate human being is halted until you start befriending again.

Behavior—Good manners learned early may bring a good job later when you are being interviewed for a job and you put your good manners to use.

Behind-the-scenes—Some of the world's most talented people are those working behind the scenes of any major event going on.

Belch—Learn to do this quietly. If you do it loudly, people will remember you for the slob you are.

Believe—Believe in God, that will keep you going, because without it you don't have anything to hold on to on your journey through life.

Bell—Groups that ring bells for music know what the word music means.

Bell, Alexander Graham—Bell's invention is now simple, but in the future you will have to make sure you have makeup and the right clothes on. Birthday suits will be out.

Bell-bottom—Bring back bell-bottom trousers and watch the good times roll with dancers galore.

Bellhop—A very important job, because their attitude will set the stage whether a guest enjoys their stay at a hotel or not.

Bellwether—Predicts the winner, but after the winner gets in, you wish the bell would have gone off one less time.

Bellyache—Don't bellyache too much, because if you ever get the real thing it won't be so funny.

Belly flop—Some people should try this into a swimming pool. It might knock some sense into them.

Belly laugh—Good to have so don't be afraid to laugh. Americans need laughter now more than ever.

Bellow—Wherever you are, that is where you belong. Make it a better place for those who will remain after you are gone.

Below the belt—Below the belt tactics is how some politicians get elected.

Bench—Sometimes your greatest players are the ones on the bench. They have played over and over again in their mind what they would do if allowed to play the game. Given the chance, they will—More than likely prove themselves talented.

Bend—Bend the rules if it means survival for someone.

Benediction—Sometimes we need this more than a shot in the arm or a vitamin.

Benefactor—If you have the money to give to those in need, do it. Maybe then the needy can do the same someday for somebody else when he or she is back on his or her feet.

Benefit of the doubt—Give yourself this if it does mean your survival in today's world.

Benign—Nice to hear, but don't forget those people who hear the other word malignant, which is a matter of life and death.

Bequeath—Leave something to somebody that will add to their quality as a human being, not something that will add greed to their heart.

Bereaved—Suffering the loss of a loved one is hard. But remember if they led a good life, they are in heaven with Our Lord.

Beret—Whatever you feel like wearing, do it. The style and the choice is yours, so don't let anyone take this away from you.

Berlin—The wall came down, but the walls that block equality for some of mankind still remain in some parts of the world.

Bermuda—Some people go here when it gets too cold for them back home. If you can't afford to go, you always have the warmth of your loved ones to help you make it through the winter.

Bermuda shorts—No matter what kind of shape your legs are, if you enjoy wearing shorts, wear them. If somebody doesn't like the look of your legs, he or she should look the other way.

Berserk—Don't go berserk over something when controlling your temper would achieve much more.

Beside—When somebody says he or she is upset over something and is beside himself or herself, that is not true. You can't come out of your own body and stand beside yourself.

Besiege—If you are besieged by problems, remember prayers can help. Also, your will power can give you the strength to overcome your problems. So don't give up hope. Our lord is standing beside you to help through your ordeal.

Best—Sometimes the ones who finish last are the best. Maybe they did the best they could with the talent they had.

Best friend—The feeling of belonging is what life is all about. But don't feel bad if you are left out in the dark by the so-called, "in crowd." Sometimes your best friend in life is yourself and doing the best you can with the realization of that.

Best man—Pick the strongest man you can find in order to catch you, in case you faint.

Bestseller—The best in life is not on the bestseller list. Sometimes things from the heart account for more.

Bet—If you bet yourself out of house and home, remember you still have the ground to walk and sleep on.

Bethlehem—The birthplace of Jesus. What greater thing can you say about a town.

Betray—Don't betray those close to your heart, because once you lose them, they may be lost forever.

Better—Be better than you are and you will see a future for yourself far better than before.

Better half—The one who stays loyal when the chips are down and in all odds.

Between—Never come between a husband and a wife, no matter which one yearns for you or you for one of them.

Beverly Hills—Where the rich and famous live. I hope they remember the poor, needy and homeless in their day to day living.

Beware—If the crime rate keeps going up, "Beware of Dog" signs may soon become, "Beware of Any Human."

Bewilder—A child cleaning his or her room can do this to many parents. Let's hope the parents do the same to their children by saying, "I love you" when they least expect it.

Beyond—Don't be afraid to go beyond the horizon. The rewards will be great if you are willing to take the chance.

Bibs—Have some handy in your house for those guests who shovel their food down.

Bible—Study it and live it. Read it even if you don't understand it. You won't walk alone through a storm if you have the knowledge of the bible with you.

Bible belt—This region tries to hold up the rest of the nation's pants.

Biceps—It's all right to exercise to get big muscles, but don't overdo it so much that you look like King Kong's cousin.

Bicker—Life is too short, so don't waste your time on being a bickerer when a peacemaker would fit your lifestyle so much better.

Bicycle—Try to ride one every day. It is good exercise.

Bid—Don't fret if you aren't the highest bidder for an item you wanted at an auction. The money you saved can be used for a higher priority: for you and your family.

Bigamy—You've heard of "three is a crowd," but with some people it's their cup of tea.

Big Ben—The Queen of England would probably like this for her own, but it is too heavy for her to carry on her wrist.

Big Bertha—The Mount Rushmore of mouths.

Big Brother—Be one when the need is there, and you'll appreciate what's in store for you.

Big Dipper—Nowadays you don't know when somebody mentions the Big Dipper if they mean something in the sky or what's going on in the dance floor.

Big house—Why is it that some of the world's biggest criminals are walking the street and some innocent people are in prison?

Big top—A good place to take your children for entertainment and to appreciate the talents of the people performing.

Bigwig—You might be a bigwig today, but watch out, for tomorrow you might be a little twig.

Bikini—Some women shouldn't wear a bikini because they are too heavy. But they shouldn't give up. They should go to their doctor and get a diet and some diet medicine. In a few months with their will power and determination, they will lose their weight and wearing a bikini will become a reality for them.

Bill—Don't overuse your charge accounts; otherwise, you will get too many bills. If you have trouble paying yours, see a financial advisor.

Billionaire—I don't care how much money you have, you still only get one day at a time like everybody else. You can only drive one car at a time, you can only wear one set of clothes at a time, and you can only live in one house at a time. Face it: there are some things money can't buy, like more than one day at a time, peace of mind and good health.

Bill of rights—The color of a person's skin doesn't enter into play here, which can't be said for everything which is a shame.

Binge—Don't drive after a drinking binge, because life behind bars is nothing to write home about.

Bingo—Playing this game with other people, can take your loneliness away.

Binocular—Live your life according to the size you can handle, and leave the other sizes to the people who were trained for them.

Biography—Write your own life story, because you are the one living it and the best judge of yourself.

Biology—Your children should take this course in high school, even if they don't like it, because it is life no matter how you slice it.

Biopsy—Don't be afraid to have a biopsy, if it's a matter of life and death. The sooner you have it done, the sooner the healing process can begin.

Birch—A beautiful tree to have in your backyard. It reminds you of the north woods.

Bird—Don't you wish you could fly like one? Instead of walking away from your troubles, you could fly away.

Birdbrain—When the canary in some people becomes a reality.

Birdcall—Make this sound, and you would be surprised how many humans even answer to it.

Bird dog—Treat this animal kindly, not something just trained to do your dirty work.

Birdhouse—Being in the birdhouse is for the husband who does something that requires worse punishment than being in the doghouse.

Bird's-eye view—If the only tickets you can get for a game are ones with a bird's eye view, go for it. A winning attitude among the team must also be present with the fans for success. So don't let your distance from your team destroy your attitude.

Birth control pill—Sex should be saved for marriage. The pill shouldn't be an excuse for teenagers to have sex. It should only be an option for married people to use.

Birthday—Remember this day as a celebration of your life, not as a remembrance of how old you are getting.

Birthday suit—They say the best things in life are free. But for this you pay a price if you see a person in a birthday suit who is out of shape.

Birth defect—A child of God to be loved and cared for just like all the other children of God born with birth defects. The parents should not get discouraged. With God's help the child can live a normal life. All he or she needs is the love of parents and the child will do all right.

Birthmark—Parents shouldn't be ashamed if their baby has a birthmark on his or her face. Sometimes the birthmark is more of a beauty mark. If the parents see it the other way as ugly and disturbing, I am sure it can be removed with surgery when the baby gets a little older. I am sure with a little loving care the baby and the parents will do all right. If the birthmark can't be removed with surgery, the parents should love that baby that much more. As time marches everything will be all right.

Bisexual—Liking both sexes. I suppose it is better than liking one and hating the other, but maybe you should limit your sexual activity to members of the opposite sex.

Bison—Protect them because they are a link to the past.

Bit—Do your bit for making life better for others, and before your life is over, you will have played a king-sized role for the betterment of mankind.

Bitch—Believe it or not, there are some of these in the world.

Bite—If you catch your child biting another child, stop them from doing it and tell them that to be a member of good standing in your family, no biting is allowed.

Bit part—Sometimes a person with a bit part in a play or movie, gets more laughs than the stars. So don't downplay the importance of a person with a bit part in a play or movie.

Bitter—Don't be bitter about something that can be replaced by laughter or love.

Bittersweet—On your honeymoon night your new bride wears a nightgown that covers her from head to toe.

Bizarre—A couple who are naked and having sex in public.

Black—Opposite of white, but just as good.

Black and blue—You get this way if Mr. Whipple catches you squeezing the Charmin.

Black and white—To some people something may not seem like black and white, it may seem like purple and orange. As long as they understand what is laid out before them, don't knock their color scheme.

Blackbelt—This can be taken two ways: either a rank in judo or karate or a belt which holds your pants up. The moral of the story is: if you intend to fool around, don't let your pants down at the wrong time or place unless you know judo or karate to protect yourself. There is no fury like an irate husband if you get caught, especially if he is six foot four and two hundred and fifty pounds.

Blackbird—This reminds me of the song, "Bye, Bye, Blackbird." If we could only pack up our care and woe and put them away and take off for a while with our families to Disney World. Let the commercial, "I'm going to Disney World," be a reality for everyone.

Blackboard—The greatest teacher in the world and also the greatest weapon in the world. If war breaks out, take a blackboard along and rub that chalk across the board. Watch the enemy take cover.

Blackeye—Not a popular color for an eye, especially if you get the worst of a disagreement.

Black-eyed Susan—A beautiful name for a flower that sparkles.

Black Hills—What greater proof that there is a God than the Black Hills and Mount Rushmore.

Blackjack—Fun to play, but don't lose your shirt over it.

Blacklist—You may be on a blacklist on earth, but in reality you may be on God's all-star list.

Blackmail—Honesty is always the best policy, then you don't have to worry about this being done to you.

Black Sheep—Whoever you consider a black sheep is maybe our lord's lost sheep, and he will rejoice when they return to the fold.

Blacksmith—A wonderful trade. Let's hope it is never forgotten.

Blame—When you are at fault, admit it, but don't let it hinder you.

Bland—Somebody or something may seem bland and dull, but the support you receive from them may well outweigh what they lack in excitement.

Blank check—Don't let your life be like a blank check. Be sure you know who and what you are responsible for.

Blasphemy—Don't speak of God in an irreverent or impious manner. God sent down His only son to die on the cross for you. Salvation from sin was made possible through Jesus' sacrifice. You should get on your hands and knees everyday to thank God for the sacrifice His son made for you on the cross.

Blast-off—Some people's mouths do this everyday while talking.

Bleachers—The bleachers at a game may not be the best place to sit, but the bleacher sitters are the heart of the team.

Bleak—If the weather outside is cold and dreary, you don't have to feel that way. You are in charge of the climate of your inner self.

Bleeding heart—It's all right to be one of these as long as you leave enough blood for your own lifeline of support.

Blend—In order for the world to survive we have to blend in as human beings, no matter what color each individual is.

Blessings—The people who make others happy when they are depressed.

Blind—People who are blind can see more than people who have their sight. When you are forced to use your imagination, you gain a type of vision not seen through your eyes.

Blind Date—Don't be afraid to go out on a blind date. A lot of blind dates lead to setting dates for marriage.

Blindfold—If you are ever in a hostage situation and you are blindfolded, remember to let your mind be your eyes and light of the world. The mind is the greatest survival kit we have in a critical situation.

Blindman's bluff—Don't play this while driving a car. Keep your eyes open and don't try to keep pace with the next person's speed. Go at the speed you know will be safe for you and your passengers.

Blink—Some towns are so small, when you drive through them, if you blink, you miss them. Their crime rate is the same way; if you blink you don't see any crime because they don't have any in some places, which is why the value of a town should be based on the quality of life in it not the size of it.

Blizzard—You can survive one of these if you use your head.

Blockhead—Some people act this way and they shouldn't because they have the ability to do better.

Blood Bank—Thank God for those who donate to a blood bank.

Bloodhound—We need more dogs like this with a keen sense of smell. They are used in tracking escaped prisoners, fugitives, etc. I think they almost give the police a run for their money. They are still only animals but I think we should appreciate them for the good and hard work they do. We should be kind to all animals even if they do nothing but lay on a couch all day.

Blood money—This kind of money if paid to the killer to commit a murder is not green like regular money. Subconsciously it is red, tainted with guilt forever until it is burned by the U.S. Treasury for being worn out. If it is money paid as compensation to the next of kin of a murdered person, it should not be called blood money. The victim's life is priceless. No amount of money can make up for the victim's life. Out of respect for the victim, they should come up with a different name for it. But for the killer, the money he gets paid is blood money, no matter how you put it.

Blood Pressure—Too much pressure in your life and this can go up. So take time out from your life once in a while to catch your breath and enjoy your family and nature.

Bloodshot—Sometimes too much partying gives you bloodshot eyes, then the girls won't want to pursue you. People will say, "He never got married, that bloodshot fool."

Bloody Mary—Drink too many of these, and you become dirty Harry or Mischievous Lily.

Bloom—Bloom where you are planted. From wherever you live, you can make a difference to the whole world if you do the best you can.

Bloomers—Bring them back and let a man's imagination have a workout for a change, because after they see Paris how are you going to keep them down on the farm?

Blooper—If you make one of these, don't take it too seriously, because it might bring much needed laughter to others.

Blot—It's nice to be able to blot out painful memories from your mind. Just be sure a segment of your life isn't lost forever.

Blow-by-blow—Some people are sticklers for details at a game, other people just want to know the outcome no matter how it's reached. The long and short of the story is: so long as you know the outcome, your style of attention to the game is yours to appreciate, no matter what anybody else thinks.

Blubber—Too much makes you overweight, so slim down and become a healthier you for the whole world to enjoy.

Blue—Let blue stand for your favorite color, not how you feel.

Bluebird—You know nature is alive and well when you see a bluebird.

Blueblood—Everybody is born equal, whether you are blueblood or not.

Blue Chip—The greatest possession of all is when you have blue chip health.

Blue-collar—The heart and soul of America are blue-collar workers. They aren't afraid of getting dirty, because their blood, sweat, and tears is the foundation America stands on.

Blue Ribbon—Make your goal in life to win a blue ribbon for being yourself the best you know how.

Bluff—It's all right to bluff your way through a poker game, but in the game of life, play it straight. You never know when the cards will be laid on the table and the facts will be known, whether you are for real or a bluff.

Blunder—Don't let a foolish mistake stop you from a productive life. Pick yourself up and go on.

Boarding School—Sometimes children are sent here for the wrong reason. For parents to send their children off just to get them out of the way means a lack of love. Children are to be treated…like the children of God they are. They should be loved and cared for. Children are precious. Parents should realize this and instead of sending their children off to boarding school, they should love and care for them with their whole heart and soul.

Boast—Don't boast so much about yourself that you can't see your own feet.

Boat—We are all in the same boat, but we all row differently from one another.

Bobby—A brave person no matter how you slice it.

Bobby Soxer—A beautiful term from a beautiful era.

Bobcat—A dangerous creature but let's try to preserve them anyway.

Body—Keep yours in shape and if you ever have to strip you won't be so embarrassed.

Body Bag—Remember the members of the U.S. Armed Forces that were put in body bags after being killed in the wars. They fought for freedom for us. Don't forget them. Say some prayers for them and their families when you think of them.

Bodybuilding—Some people think they need a body workout and other people desire to go to a think tank seminar. But the smartest people of all are those who accept what they have to work with and do the best they can.

Bodyguard—We all have our own bodyguard; our guardian angel looks after us.

Body search—A policeman searching a woman suspect is okay as long as he does a proper search and doesn't keep his hands in one spot too long, like her breasts.

Body Shop—Hunt for a good one for your car. When you find it, hang on to it. Take your car there regularly. A good body shop is worth a million dollars.

Bogeyman—This doesn't have to be real as long as you remember being scared; isn't a weakness, it's a growth process of life.

Boiling Point—It's all right to bring water to a boil, just make sure your temper doesn't reach this point all the time.

Bold—Be bold when you have to, but don't make a habit of trampling over people to get ahead in life.

Bomb—One going off is one too many. The world needs peace now more than ever.

Bombshell—The Democratic and Republican parties both come clean and there is no more dirty campaigns.

Bond—Buy U.S. Savings Bonds and help keep America on top of the world.

Bondage—Lincoln freed the slaves, but the way some people's jobs and marriages are, bondage is a person wonders.

Bone—Beauty is just skin deep, so make sure bones are healthy.

Bonehead—Somebody who is made to sit in the corner at school and can't keep the dunce cap on because he or she puts it on wrong and tries to balance it on his or her head. Also, somebody who drives wrong on a one-way street and then tries to go with the flow of the traffic by driving in reverse.

Bone to pick—Be sure if you have a bone to pick with somebody, you have the backbone to back yourself up.

Bonfire—A nice homecoming event, so don't let booze spoil it.

Bonkers—You could go bonkers when you use a public toilet and a little breeze keeps blowing off the paper you use to line the seat with. Also, when the seat won't stay down for you to line it.

Bonnet—Wear one if you like it, because it's your head and you should wear what becomes you no matter what anybody else thinks.

Bonus—Don't judge your job by how big of a bonus you get. Judge it by how many people you make happier because of it.

Boo—Don't boo anybody or anything unless you can do better.

Booby prize—A trip to the Caribbean Islands on the Titanic II.

Booby trap—Your girlfriend's ex-husband is six foot four, three hundred pounds, and very jealous of her, and he has a temper.

Bookkeeping—A good job, because you help keep the world in balance.

Bookmobile—Be sure you support the bookmobile. It is important for your children's education. Especially during the summer when the school library is closed. Also, if your town doesn't have a library. As a parent, you can get good use from it too. You can become more knowledgeable about things and pass on what you learned to your children. So appreciate and support the bookmobile as it travels around the country.

Book Review—Don't let other people's critical appraisal of your book stop you from getting your foot in the door of the publishing world. What you think of your book will get you inside the door, not what other people think.

Bookstore—Some of the best books are not in bookstores. They are unwritten ones that some people say they don't have the talent to write, but they do.

Boombox—If you are a teenager or even an adult show some courtesy for other people and don't play this so loud that you awake the dead.

Boomerang—Life is like a boomerang; the more good you do, the more good feelings about yourself will come back to you.

Boondocks—Don't be ashamed to admit you live in the hinterlands. After all, that is where nature is the most beautiful.

Boot Camp—If you can survive this, you can survive anything.

Bootleg—People pay good money for CDs and tapes. It isn't right that some people bootleg CDs and tapes. This illegal act should be stopped and the guilty parties punished. Just think of the innocent people who buy these CDs and tapes. They are not guilty of anything except for being hardworking people who work hard for their money. God bless them for that.

Border—Even if guards stop you at a border crossing, they can't stop your spirit from reaching heights you never dreamed of.

Boring—If you are bored with your life, go to a nursing home or an orphanage and do some volunteer work. When you go home, you will appreciate the difference. Also, this happens when you aren't using all your God-given talents. Research your mind and see what you come up with new.

Born-Again—You don't have to be a born-again Christian to have a commitment to Jesus Christ. Just recycle the basics you were taught and apply it to a level you can understand, and your commitment to Jesus Christ will be an enjoyable experience.

Borrow—Be sure to return that which belongs to another, because a reputation of returning on time will insure future borrowing for yourself.

Boss—A good one appreciates, a bad one ignores. What a good one says is knowledge for your mind. What a bad one says is trash, so in one ear and out the other with it.

Bossy—Don't let a bossy person get the best of you. The sunshine you create inside of you is far greater force than his or her domineering output.

Boston—This city is packed with history. Go and visit it someday.

Boston Cream Pie—Good to eat and an ideal weapon in a pie fight.

Boston Rocker—Relax in one once in a while or in any other type of rocker, it does the heart good.

Botany—Take care of your plants, because they are the booster-uppers you need.

Bother—Don't make a pest of yourself unless it is for a good cause.

Bottle—Bottle up your good memories and let them out when you are feeling sad.

Bottom—From this position the only thing to do is ascend.

Bottomless—Some people's stomachs are this, and they pay for it with their Texas spread.

Bouncer—A tough job because you have to watch out that the people you are bouncing at don't bounce back on you.

Bound—Be prepared to go home someday. It's the reward you deserve if you live right.

Boundary—Don't limit yourself as a human being. Learn as much as you can and watch the power of your mind grow.

Bounty hunter—Too bad sometimes it takes a reward for the apprehension of a criminal. Let justice be served and goodness reign supreme. Let's hope it doesn't depend upon whether the price is right or not.

Bourbon—If you drink too much of this, don't go anywhere until you can see straight again.

Bout—Never give up the struggle through life. Strength is gained when you put up a fight.

Boutiques—Better than a large store because you can buy city styles in a small town flavor.

Boutonniere—Good for a man to wear to dress up a suit jacket or a sports jacket. It's not considered feminine for a man to wear a boutonniere and if it is, who the hell gives a damn. Isn't it time once and for all that we quit this position that a woman should wear this and a man should wear that. Whether you are a man or a woman, wear what you want. It's nobody's business but your own what you wear.

Bowl—Years ago some parents would use a bowl upside down to cut their children's hair. Nowadays some of the kids' hair looks like a bowl right side up.

Bowlegged—If some people make fun of you because of this, don't let them bother you. Better to have bowlegs than a spacey mind like some of the people making fun of you do.

Bowling Alley—Sometimes there is more action going on with the spectators than on the lanes.

Bowtie—I think this is easier to wear than a necktie. The clip-ons are easy to put on. Years ago I think the image of a bowtie were men who were square and who wore glasses wore bowties. That was just my thinking. Maybe it isn't true at all. Now bowties are first class, they are worn with tuxedos.

Box—If you have to stand on a box to give yourself some height, don't feel bad. In order to sit on top of the world, it doesn't matter what you use as a stepping stone.

Box Car—Bedroom for some people, whom some people would call America's undesirables but in God's world, they are called priority ones.

Boxer Shorts—I think more women want men to wear briefs than boxer shorts. I think they believe men who wear briefs are sexier.

Boxing Gloves—Some women in their marriages take much physical abuse, they would be better off to wear a pair of these daily for protection.

Box Seat—No matter what you pay for a seat, everybody sees and hears the same entertainment. The size of the entertainer or entertainers may be different, but the talent remains the same.

Boycott—Don't boycott anybody or anything that will hurt your livelihood too.

Boyfriend—If your boyfriend props you, don't feel bad. For every man who doesn't know how to treat a lady, there is a gentleman who does. Be patient and you will meet your Mr. Right.

Boy Scouts—A beautiful training ground to teach young men and boys about the good they can spread in the world. A lot of places where there is good in the world today instead of bad, it is because of former boy scouts living there.

Bra Burner—I wonder if women still do this. If they do, it's nobody's business but their own. The feminist movement is a part of history. It shouldn't be condemned. The women in this movement believed in the social, political, and economic equality of the sexes. This is America. They are entitled to their views. That can't be taken away from them because they are part of history forever. Men and women are created equal. They should be treated the same. Especially in job pay. If they do the same job, they should get the same pay. A woman shouldn't be held back from any job she wants.

Brace—Don't be ashamed to wear one, if you need one. It is there to help you, not hinder you.

Brag—Be careful that you don't brag too much, eating crow might be around the corner.

Braille, Louis—God bless him for inventing a writing and printing system for visually impaired or sightless people.

Brainpower—Use whatever brainpower you have got. It isn't the quantity that counts, but the quality.

Brainstorm—Be careful of some brainstorms, they may turn out to be brain calm.

Brake—When it comes to sin, do this.

Branch—Spread out and see how much you can learn.

Brand—It isn't the trademark that counts; it's the quality of performance.

Brand-new—Don't worry if you don't have a lot of brand-new things. The memories you have of your old things count more.

Brass knuckles—People fighting with their bare knuckles is bad enough, but brass knuckles are something that should have never seen the light of day.

Brass tacks—Sometimes getting down to brass tacks is the only way you can make the brass realize you are for real.

Brave—You are bold and willing to face danger, pain or trouble. You may not think you are this, but when the time comes, with God's help, you will find it in yourself.

Brawl—Avoid this, and if you see one call the police.

Breach of promise—If you are left standing at the altar, don't feel bad. You are still better off than Mary Ann sitting at the seashore shifting sand. Be patient, alert, and bright, and your knight in shining armor will come through the door. Instead of a sword and shield in his hand, he will have an "I do."

Bread and Butter—Don't downplay the importance of your job. As long as you bring home the bread and butter, don't concern yourself with how fancy your table setting is.

Breadline—We have this even today. Let's hope for the day when the only thing people are waiting in line for is to go to church.

Breadwinner—If you are the breadwinner, be appreciative of the ones keeping your home fires burning while you are on the job.

Break—Don't break a heart.

Breakaway—Break away from your bad habits and restart your engine to accomplish your life's goals.

Breakdown—Don't let a breakdown get the best of you. Sometimes it takes a major fall to build the strength for a new beginning.

Breakfast—A good breakfast is the only way to start a day. Start on an empty stomach, and nasty growls become your constant companion.

Breaking point—If you experience this, bounce back and start a mending point.

Breakthrough—When a computer is made that everyone in the world can understand.

Breastfeed—Some men never outgrow their desire for this.

Breathless—It will make you breathless if the person elected president of the United States keeps all the promises he or she made during the campaign.

Breathing—God's love for you.

Breeze—Make sure you remind people of a cool breeze, instead of a hot air balloon.

Breezeway—Nice place to relax and discuss the issues of the world.

Brewery—Nice place to work if your personal high comes from your paycheck and not from the samples you drink.

Bribery—Get caught doing this, and you will probably be singing, "jailhouse rock" better than Elvis did.

Bricklayer—They are the person who work hard for their money. In the summer they sweat from the heat and in the winter they freeze from the cold. They are skilled in building with bricks. Nobody should be envious of the money they make. They deserve every cent they get.

Bride—There shouldn't be any homely women in this world, because whenever somebody goes to a wedding, they always say the bride looks so beautiful.

Bridesmaids—Remember the saying, "Always a bridesmaid, never a bride?" That's not so bad. A lot of the bridesmaids are cuter than the brides.

Bridge—To keep the bridge over your troubled waters firm and strong, remember to eat right, exercise and get enough sleep. You are always going to have problems. You just have to have the strength and will to overtake them.

Bridgework—It should be called skyscraper work for the amount you have to pay for it.

Brief—Let me be brief, your performance in bed depends on you. The color of your briefs or how sexy they are has nothing to do with it.

Briefcase—Just because you don't carry a briefcase to work doesn't mean your job isn't important. It's what you do with your hands, not what you carry, that counts.

Bright—For a man it's marrying a woman three times his size and charging her by the pound for rent. For a woman it's marrying a man three times her size and charging him so much a square foot to get around him.

Bring—It doesn't matter who brings home the bacon, so long as somebody brings it. If nobody can bring home the bacon in your home, don't be afraid to accept assistance. That's what it's there for.

Brink—The brink of discovery for you could be your mind. Discovering the secret of it could mean a greater learning base. The more you learn, the more you progress as a human being, which means one more plus for the world.

Britain—I wouldn't want to live in this country, because the monarchy stays in the same family. At least in this country we get a change for sure every eight years.

Broadcast—Broadcast your voice at a volume that will increase good in the world rather than decrease it.

Broad Jump—It isn't how far you can jump that counts in life, it's that you can get your feet off the ground.

Broadminded—Be broad-minded if it will free you from being prejudiced.

Broadway—Some of the best plays in the world don't even make it to Broadway.

Brokenhearted—After your heart has healed, you will find a heart that is stronger and able to cope better should another crisis arise in your life.

Broker—Pick out a good one because they are shaping your future.

Bronze—It means third place in competition but it doesn't have to mean the same in your heart. Maybe you gave a first place effort according to your ability, so remember it as such.

Broom—Life is like sweeping dirt off a floor, you can sweep the dirt away, but you still have the floor to deal with. In other words, every time it gets dirty you have to sweep it.

Brotherhood—We all belong to the brotherhood of God. I wish everybody would act like it towards one another.

Browbeat—Don't let a bully spoil your disposition. Think of people who cheer you up rather than people who would sooner stick a pin to a balloon than blow one up.

Brownout—Use electricity wisely, otherwise can darkness be far behind?

Brush-off—Don't worry if somebody gives you the brush-off. The quicker you learn in life not to let people bother you, the better off you will be.

Bubble—If someone breaks yours, blow up another one.

Bubble Bath—If tension is getting the best of you, take a bubble bath. Do this every day or whenever you can find the time and you will find yourself relaxed day in and day out.

Bubble gum—Blow a bubble to show that life can be fun no matter how old you are.

Buck—Whether you pass the buck or stop the buck, be sure you save some of the buck. In your later years, it will come in handy to live on.

Bucket seats—Tough to have sex in.

Buckingham Palace—Where people are waited on hand and foot and then some.

Buckle—Buckle up for safety, because if you don't, maybe someday you won't have any need for that other belt.

Bud—Take care of this and see the beautiful flower you can have.

Buddhism—Let people believe in the religion they want; whatever gives them internal peace, it's their business, nobody else's.

Buddy—Be this to somebody who has no one else.

Budget—You may have to live on a budget, but the best thing in life still is free to enjoy: nature.

Buff—Make sure if you swim in the buff you have the body for it. Out of shape people who swim in the buff are hard on the eyes.

Buggy—When you see how fast some of the cars are driven on the freeway, a person almost wishes the horse and buggy would come back. We would have to watch where we step, but at least the beauty of the horses would be worth the loss of time.

Build—Develop the strength inside of you and when you need it, reach down and use it with all the gusto you have.

Builder—They make somewhere over the rainbow a reality for first time homeowners.

Building—A person can bomb a building, but they can't destroy the principles of the people who occupied that building.

Bulb—When the bulb between your ears goes out, be sure you replace it. Put in a bigger one. You never outgrow your need for knowledge.

Bull—Some people take the bull by the horns and other people can throw a bull by the tail. Some people like to watch a bull go by and other people run like hell when they see a bull. The moral of the story is: don't judge yourself by the bull in your life.

Bulldog—Maybe not the most beautiful dog in the world, but the joy they bring to people more than makes up for it.

Bulldozer—Don't be too eager to bulldoze a building. Think of the history behind it.

Bullet—A bullet is powerless without a gun, and a gun is powerless without a hand. Let's learn to control all three.

Bully—Don't show your colors by being a bully. If you want to show your colors, do an oil painting.

Bum—What we save money for to become someday.

Bumper Sticker—If you see a car with a sign saying, "Nerd on Board," that means there is a nerd inside sitting on a piece of lumber.

Bungalow—Don't compare a bungalow to a mansion, because what one lacks in size is made up by the warmth and cozy feeling that exists inside.

Bunkbed—A nightmare for a honeymoon couple when they find out they only room left at the hotel they have a reservation has bunk beds only.

Bunt—Probably the greatest hit in baseball. It doesn't only depend on how you hit the ball, but also if you advance the base runner.

Buoyancy—Make a habit of it and hope that this habit is picked up by others.

Burden—Don't be a burden when, with just a little effort on your part, you could be uplifting people's spirits.

Burger—A poor man's steak but a good one; no other food can touch it with a ten-foot pole.

Burglar—They steal what people have earned through hard work.

Burial—You can bury the body, but the soul is free like an eagle forever.

Burlesque—Bring it back and let the good times roll.

Burn—Don't let scars from a fire destroy you. You exist through the internal you, no matter what people think of the external you. So think good thoughts and be good to yourself and you will make it through the night.

Burnout—If this happens to you, don't let it bother you. Get your rest and then recharge yourself and go up the hill again.

Bus—They say relax and leave the driving to us. Let's hope the criminal element drive their own cars and let the bus and passengers travel in peace.

Busboy—They clear the way for a more enjoyable meal for all.

Bush League—Out of the minors will come the majors of tomorrow.

Business—If you own a business, be sure you have the best help you can get. Kind and courteous salespeople will do more for your business than new merchandise, a new store or even a remodeled store.

Business Card—Be sure you check out the person who hands you this. A business card is no guarantee they represent what is on the card and that you will get the best deal in town.

Business College—Some people go to college to learn business. Other people learn it through the everyday experience of dealing with humanity.

Busybody—They fill their dull lives by concerning themselves with other people's business.

Butcher—To a vegetarian, their meat is a nightmare. To other people their meat is a mouthwatering delight.

Butler—He opens the door for people, and I think he would sooner give some of them a swift kick in the caboose.

Butter—Don't butter up people too much, because somebody might margarine you down someday.

Butterfingers—If you are a person who tends to drop things, don't feel bad. You work with your hands the best you know how. Practice makes perfect. I am sure if you practice using your hands handling objects, you will get over this habit of dropping objects. Just hand in there. You will be all right.

Butterfly—Let this be a symbol of being free, not a symbol of an uneasy feeling in one's stomach. I have never seen a butterfly fly out of a person's mouth yet. Butterflies are beautiful, give them the credit due to them.

Butterfly stroke—It doesn't matter if you can't do the fancy strokes and the belly flop is your style. Swim for the enjoyment of it.

Butterscotch—Treat yourself to this when you are feeling down on your luck and want an uplifting feeling from a sensational taste.

Button—A small item, but one of the greatest inventions in the world.

Buttonhole—Thank God for those people who believe silence is golden unless they have something important to say.

Buyers' market—It's a buyers' market until it's over, then you need to own Fort Knox to buy anything.

Buzz—It's okay to tell a person who happens to be a pest to buzz off until they come by again, then you have to bring out the pest spray.

Buzzard—Mascot of the people who gather once a month and smile just once to see what it is like.

BYOB—It's all right to go to a BYOB (Bring Your Own Bottle) party, but be sure you can BYOB (Bring Yourself On Back) when it comes time to go home.

Bypass—Don't be ashamed to avoid something you fear. Practice your strengths, and the next time you won't have to bypass your fears.

Byword—Try to reason out and solve your own problems. It may be blood, sweat, and tears, but success will be your byword.

C

Cab—Better to hail a cab than Hitler.

Cabaret—The place to go to for food and live entertainment. Go there if the entertainment is good and clean. If the entertainment is dirty, don't go. Don't fill your mind with filth because there is enough filth in this world already. I am talking about dirty books, movies, magazines, television, etc.

Cabdriver—Appreciate them; they have a dangerous job.

Cabin—A place to go and let your troubles float away on the lake or river or whatever.

Cabin boy—When you go on a cruise, sometimes the cabin boy will light your fire more than the scenery will.

Cabin cruiser—Another name for it is a floating waterbed.

Cabinet—Sometimes your cabinet at home is more active than the cabinet in the White House.

Cabin Fever—Another name for it is spouse burnt-out.

Cable Television—If it gets any more sexy, it will be arrested for indecent exposure.

Caboose—It may be at the rear, but it will be remembered because it is the last thing you see when the train goes by.

Cactus—Put this under the seat of a slow riser.

Caddie—I think golfers should carry their own clubs. With the extra strength built up by carrying their own load, they could hit the ball farther.

Cadets—Cadets make me think of west point, the place they go to learn how to be brave when it comes to defending freedom for the rest of us to enjoy.

Caesar Salad—This was Julius Caesar's favorite salad. I wonder why?

Café—In the wintertime when your rich friends are in a warm state and you are in a cold one, treat yourself to a cup of coffee and a donut. A warm climate is whatever the heart desires it to be.

Cage—A lot of animals in cages have a stronger will to live than even some humans. When freedom is taken away, the determination to regain it provides the spark needed to survive.

Cake—With some people you would bake a cake if you knew they were coming, but with some others you would sooner lock the deadbolt on the door.

Cakewalk—The rich person's version of this is Mercedes run.

Calculate—Don't calculate your money before you have earned it.

Calendar—No matter what month or year it is, every day is different. So live for today, because yesterday is gone and tomorrow does not yet belong to us.

California—Where the movie stars are, but you can be one right where you are. Everybody's a star in the movie of their life.

Call—Call someone far away and let them know you care.

Callback—Make sure when a product is called back for safety reasons, you take it back. Your family can't be replaced.

Calligraphy—Practice this, because once it is learned, you can make people happy by writing letters in this style.

Calling Card—Make sure when you leave your calling card somewhere, the welcome mat is still out when you make a return visit.

Callous—Some people get this way when life deals them a bad hand of cards. They just have to learn to reshuffle the hand and cut the cards and deal.

Calm—You have heard of the calm before the storm. What counts even more is how calm you are after the storm.

Calorie—Don't feel bad if you are counting calories to lose some weight. You are not alone. Many people are doing this. Just think of that and you will win the battle of the bulge. Just be patient and pounds will come off.

Camel—Be like a camel: store something in your heart and let it pour forth when the need is there.

Camelot—I think when President Kennedy was in the White House and Jacqueline Kennedy was First Lady, they called it Camelot. I think it was. I miss it.

Cameo—You may think your role in life is small, but in God's eyes nobody can play your part in life better than you can.

Camera—Take pictures of people you love and if any of them dies, remember the love you had for them from the pictures.

Camouflage—Don't hide your true feelings when it comes to living your life. It is only through truth that your expression of self will be complete.

Camp—Camp isn't only for children. Give senior citizens a break by taking them to a camp for days of relaxation away from the tensions and crimes of the city.

Campaign—If you campaign for a candidate and you end up with the short end of the stick, that's not so bad, because eventually it teaches you how to handle the long end of the stick when you get a hold of it.

Camper—To relax: go camping, start a campfire, roast some marshmallows and sing your heart out.

Camp Fire Girl—Good training ground to reach young ladies that spreading goodness and kindness does pay in life.

Campground—Keep it clean for the next person to enjoy.

Campus—Do your part to make campuses safer; report crime when you see it.

Can—You can do anything you want to if you remember, even in defeat you can overcome the loss at hand.

Canary—Wonderful bird to have as a pet. When they start to warble, it is beautiful. It's worth your money to buy one.

Cancan—Women entertainers should be sure to have underwear on when they do this dance. Otherwise how are you going to keep the men on the farm after they see Paris.

Cancer—Those who die from it pave the way for a cure of it.

Candelabrum—For some of the music of today, instead of a candelabrum you almost have to bring the earplugs out.

Candid—Be honest at all times, because it will reveal you are a person to be trusted.

Candid Camera—Smile at all times because you never know when Candid Camera is watching and filming.

Candle—It's better to light a candle and share it with the whole world than to curse the darkness.

Candy Striper—Their volunteer work is priceless in the amount of good they do.

Cane—Don't feel foolish to use one. It was made for the purpose of helping human beings. Don't pay any attention if somebody says something out of place. Better for you to stay on your feet than to listen to somebody saying something foolish.

Cannon—If you really want to achieve your goals in life, go after them, making the sound of a cannon instead of a cap gun.

Cannot—Let 'can do' be your battle cry, not 'cannot do'.

Canoe—In life you have to paddle your own canoe, but you get to decide how fast or slow you paddle. In other words, you choose your own speed.

Can of worms—Count your blessings if your troubles are only like a can of worms. Some people's are like an ocean of whales.

Can't—You can't take it with you because the cost of living today has it all.

Canteen—Thank God for all those who served in these during the wars. I am sure the soldiers appreciated all the help and support they got from the workers in the canteen.

Canvas—Paint whatever your heart desires, no matter if nobody else understands it.

Cap—Wear one whenever you want to, no matter what anybody else thinks.

Capacity—If you have the ability to do something better, do it. It is when you use the resources within you that the resources outside of you become better.

Cape—Wear a cape for a Halloween party or for fashion but don't make love in one. Otherwise it might end up in a caper.

Capital—Any town is capable of being the capital of a state. The townspeople just have to work at the image they want to project.

Capital Punishment—I think in some cases this is needed, because if you can't live according to the rules of society, you have given up your right to be a part of society.

Capitol Hill—Sometimes there is a hill even higher in Washington. It is known as B.S. Hill.

Capsule—In capsule form, how does your life come out? Pick out your strengths and work them to your advantage as your life goes on.

Captain—Learn to be a good follower first, then you can be a good captain.

Captive—You may be held prisoner against your will, but you still control how you react to what is done to you by others.

Car—Why do they make cars that you can drive so fast? You can't drive that fast because of the speed limit. The way some people drive, you would swear they were driving that fast.

Carat—It's a reality of life that while some people in the world are starving, some other people in the world need steel fingers in order to carry the weight from all the carats in their rings.

Carbon Copy—Why are there lawsuits when somebody copies someone else's work? They should have pride that somebody thought so much of their work that they copied it.

Car Coat—Add to nature by wearing a car coat instead of a mink. A lot of animals shouldn't have to suffer for the fashion of a few people.

Card—Send one to somebody who has nobody else.

Care—Give it to those who need it. A helping hand offered is a hand well-received and appreciated more often than not.

Career—Let your profession be what satisfies you, not the rest of the world.

Careful—As you travel through life, be careful not to take too many rest stops, otherwise your career goals will be slowed to a snail's pace.

Careless—Don't be careless when it comes to using credit cards, otherwise your cupboards might be barer than Mother Hubbard's.

Carol—Cheer somebody up, sing carols anytime of the year.

Carousel—An enjoyable and peaceful ride for one and all. If you are a child at heart, ride it. You never outgrow your need for a ride on a carousel.

Carpenter—A beautiful trade. They repair and build the wood products of the world, making it a sturdier place for all of us to live.

Car Pool—For rich people, this means they have a swimming pool for their cars.

Carrier Pigeon—Put them to good use. Between countries, to preserve peace, send a message by carrier pigeon.

Carrots—Rabbits don't wear glasses. Carrots must be good for something.

Carry—The definition of a cheap person is one who will carry their teenager in their arms in order to obtain a cheaper fare for them at a game, etc.

Car Seat—Be sure you have car seats for your young children. Also, be sure you read the directions and put in the car seats right. Your children are precious so do everything possible to make sure they have a safe car trip every time you put them in their car seats.

Cart—Grocery stores should make sure they have their grocery carts in tiptop shape especially the wheels. It is hard for senior citizens to push their carts when the wheels are going every other way. It is hard for people of every age when this happens to the wheels of the carts.

Cartoon—To relieve the pressures of life, watch a cartoon once in a while.

Cartwheel—If you feel overjoyed about something, do one in your front yard. Who cares what the neighbors think.

Car Wash—Respect those people who work in a car wash, because cleaner cars mean cheerier people as they drive down the road.

Case—When you go into court, be prepared. A case well-prepared is a case well heard.

Cashier—This is a hard job. You are on your feet all day, and you never know what kind of mood your customers will be in.

Casino—Be careful if a casino becomes your second home. Too many losses, and you may not have a first home to go back to.

Castle—You may not live in one, but be thankful you have a roof over your head.

Castro—He should shave and he might not look so hateful.

Catalog—Make sure you don't overdo when shopping from a catalog. Sometimes pay later becomes 'can't' pay because you have no cash.

Cat-and-mouse—People running for political office play this with one another. The voters should join in the fun and play hide-and-seek with them. Every time you see them coming, hide and keep your pockets covered.

Cataract—Take care of your eyes, because you don't want to miss the beauty surrounding you.

Catastrophe—Handle it the best way you know how, and with God's help you can start anew.

Catch—Catch a falling star and throw it back in the sky. Stars are meant to be shiners, not pocket occupiers.

Catch-22—You may marry for money, only to find out later your father-in-law is in prison for making counterfeit money, and your wife tells you that her daddy taught her everything she knows.

Catcher—I feel sorry for this person. He has to bend his knees during a game. He is between an opponent with a bat in his hands and a man with an inflated stomach. Also, a man who is supposed to be his friend is throwing a hard object at him.

Caterpillar—Appreciate them for the beautiful thing they turn into.

Cathedral—Go to one often and pray for peace in the world.

Cattleman—He tends your dinner, so appreciate him as you bite into your steak.

Cattle prod—Most people just need a cup of coffee to get started in the morning, but for some people you almost need a cattle prod.

Cauliflower ear—You can get this living with, working with, or going to school with a nonstop talker.

Cause—If your cause is a just one, work hard for it, because efforts well spent will pay off in a more livable world for all.

Caution—It's all right to be on guard against danger, but don't let it stop you from living. Throw caution to the wind and have some fun.

Cavalry—Some neighbors you would like to bake a cake for when they come over, while other neighbors you would like to call out the cavalry when they come.

Cave—Don't hide in one. Overcome your shyness and be a part of life.

Cave dweller—They made sacrifices so that we can enjoy the luxuries of today.

Cedar—Be sure your insulation for life is sturdy, because you are going to need it in order to survive the tough times.

Ceiling—You know the saying, "what goes up, must come down." Well, be careful of a revengeful ceiling in your house.

Celebrate—Help a friend mark a special occasion; for having a friend is worth the effort put forth for the celebration.

Cement—Sometimes during a long hot summer, it would be easier to cement over a lawn than to cut it.

Cement Factory—The mob has another name for this: shoe store.

Censor—Show concern for what your children are exposed to, because they are the world's future.

Centenarian—One hundred years old, bring on the candles. You can't bake a cake big enough to show their wealth of wisdom.

Center—May the center of your life be what gives you the most strength.

Ceramics—A good art to learn. It keeps the fingers young and thin.

Cereal—Be sure to eat breakfast in the morning, because just like a race, you need a good start to get your day off right.

Certain—Be sure of your facts before you speak. There is enough hot air in the atmosphere already.

Cesspool—People who cheat other people out of their inheritance should stink with shame.

Chain gang—Years ago, the prisoners were the chain gang, now the victims of crimes are the chain gang. This is because of the way some in law enforcement and society treat them.

Chain Letter—Don't be trapped by something you can control, unless you feel secure being dictated to by others.

Chain-smoke—Be a friend to your lungs instead of to a cigarette.

Challenge—The prospects for tomorrow depend upon how you accept the challenges of today.

Chambermaid—They are better detectives than Sherlock Holmes, so don't try any hanky-panky in the beds they make.

Chamber of Commerce—They can either make or break a city.

Champagne—Drink too much of this, and you will give the bubbly inside of the bottle competition.

Champion—Last place finishers qualify as this, too, because life goes on and so must they. It doesn't matter who's on first as long as they know their part in life and have the capacity to reach the finish line. It doesn't matter the length of time it takes them to get there. Just as long as they did it to the best of their ability who cares where they finished. They are champions in my book.

Chance—To be successful, you have to take risks. Otherwise, the enjoyment of succeeding won't be there.

Chaperone—Don't resent them for being around, because they care for your well-being and the well-being of your friends.

Chaplain—They serve to bring comfort to those away from home, like those in the armed forces.

Chandelier—Hang from one, and you'll see how the rich people play.

Change—Change what you can and accept what you can't, with the exception being that you won't give up fighting for what you believe in.

Change of Life—Be understanding when this is happening to the loved one in your life.

Chap—Chapped hands and lips mean winter, but it doesn't mean it has to stop you cold as far as outside activity goes. Put lip balm on your lips and hand lotion on your hands. Put more clothes on, enjoy yourself, and melt down winter with the time of your life.

Chapel—Pray in a chapel even when you aren't in the need of something. When you know God on a regular basis, your problems become manageable on a regular basis.

Character—This is built by appreciating the talents of others and discovering your own talents and being just as appreciative of them and using them to the best of your ability.

Charade—Don't play games. Taking on the real world is the only way you get to know life, learn life, and live life as a true human being.

Charge—Don't charge so much that when your bills come in the mail, you have to pay for them with the credit line you have left from your charge cards.

Chariot—This is probably safer than some of the cars on the road today.

Charity—Those who can't afford to give but give anyway are the most charitable people in the world.

Charm—Don't expect being charming to be the answer to all your prayers. Some things take good old elbow grease and hard work to get accomplished.

Chase—It's all right to chase a rainbow, but make sure once you catch it, you can handle it.

Chauffeur—You should be in the driver's seat of your life. Don't expect others to do the driving for you.

Cheap—You pay for what you get, so make sure the price is right.

Cheap shot—If you have one of these directed at you, don't let it derail you from your purpose in life. The truth will set you free, and you know inside that the truth is there and freedom isn't far behind.

Cheapskate—A husband who gives his wife a birthday card and tells her to give it back to him when she is done reading it so he can use it again next year.

Cheat—Shame on you if you cheated somebody out of their hard earned money. If you are a storeowner and you cheated customers by overcharging them for purchases or if you are somebody who cheated somebody out of their land, you should both go to jail.

Check—Bounce a basketball instead of a check.

Checkbook—If you can't balance your own checkbook, how do you expect somebody else to? Take responsibility for your money, you earned it, so take charge before the overdraft charges do.

Checklist—Make a list of the good and bad things in your life. If the bad things outweigh the good things it's time for you to reverse this. If you do reverse it, you will feel happier about your life and yourself. So do it for your own peace of mind.

Checkup—Get a checkup on a routine basis, otherwise your checkout time from life might be sooner than you think. This is one thing no rain check is available for.

Cheerful—If you are joyful, share it with the first sad person you meet.

Cheerleader—When the girls receive more attention than the cheers, it's time for the hemlines to be lowered.

Cheesecake—I like the kind you eat, because there's more dressing on it.

Cherish—Cherish your loved ones while you can, because when they are gone it's hard to touch a memory.

Chest—The size of your chest is not the important thing in life, it's the values you have as a human being that count.

Chestnut—Roast some any time of the year, and share some with a lonely person.

Chicken—At some doctors' offices you have to wait so long, you can count your chickens before they hatch.

Chicken Feed—I may be chicken feed in the morning, but by the time night comes along, the rooster will be crowing about it.

Chief—For a follower to become a chief, he or she needs to study the style and manners of a chief. Also, if he or she is a good chief, follow their example and someday you will be a chief of a company or something like that.

Chief Justice—He or she may be called the chief justice, but without the support of the other judges, they aren't so chief.

Chihuahua—What a cute small dog. Just right for somebody living in an apartment. Great for a homeowner too. Easy to pick up and put on your lap too. Great for small kids and big ones, too. Just a wonderful pet to have.

Childhood—Some children have hard lives, but if they hang on long enough, they will survive into adulthood. All they need for inspiration is to look at the adults who survived an unhappy childhood and now lead productive lives as adults.

Childish—A forty-year-old wanting to put a diaper on his or her teddy bear before he or she takes it to bed with him or her.

Child labor—We shouldn't have child labor in this country. We should have children thinking, where they read books instead of watching too much television.

Child's play—Sometimes a very simple task done right is the difference between life and death.

Chime—Wonderful to hear as you walk on a sidewalk in the city. Whether you hear it from a bell tower in city hall or a clock on a high buildings, it's a wonderful sound to hear.

Chimney Sweep—Too bad this person couldn't remove soot that is embedded beyond the chimney of some of the places they clean, such as drugs, child abuse, wife beating, etc.

Chimpanzee—This animal is so humanlike that it would be nice to have as a pet. It has a high degree of intelligence. The only thing it would be a mess in the house if he or she wasn't housebroken. You would have to put diapers on he or she. If you didn't like that, you would have to housebreak them.

China—Nice to eat off of, but when you are starving, the kind of plate you eat off does nothing to ease the pain in your stomach.

Chinatown—Nice way to preserve one's motherland living in a different country. Just like a group of Americans living in a certain section of a foreign country. They are preserving America in a different country.

Chinchilla—More beautiful to leave the fur on the animal than to have a person wear the fur.

Chip—Some people have a chip on their shoulder; with others it is more like a block.

Chipmunk—Alvin and the Chipmunks' songs at Christmastime, what a delight and a joy of a memory that remains in one's heart forever.

Chivalry—It's not dead; you just have to dig harder to find it.

Chocolate—One of life's finest pleasures.

Choices—Use your common sense as much as possible, and you will make the right choices in life.

Choir—Sing in one; it's good exercise for your lungs. You don't need to sell a million records in order to sing. Everybody can sing; it just sounds different to different ears.

Choker—Give one of these to a woman who talks too much. Make it a very tight one.

Chopsticks—Learn to use these and learning a computer will seem like a cakewalk.

Chord—Play your chords right, and you will be providing music for the whole world to hear.

Choreography—A beautiful and wonderful art. The pain you go through in rehearsal is well worth the applause from the audience.

Chorus—Join a chorus and spread the happiness that life can be.

Christian—Somebody who believes in Jesus as Christ or follows the religion based on the life and teachings of Jesus, whether he or she goes to church every Sunday or not. A Christian's life is not easy, but Jesus chose the path of thorns and survived. So a Christian can survive too.

Christmas—If you are alone at this time of the year, you don't have to be lonely. Celebrate our Lord's birthday on a one-to-one basis; the best way to get to know him better. Also, Christmas happens every day, because every day the rebirth of Jesus is happening in somebody's soul.

Christmas Tree—Decorate it not with how much money can buy, but with things from the heart.

Chubby—If you are chubby, don't let it spoil your fun. Just roll with your rolls or vow to get thinner if it bothers you. If you can't lose the pounds, don't fret. If you are a nice person, society needs more people like you, the way the world is today.

Chump—The way some people eat, you think they are scared somebody is going to steal their food off their plate before they are done eating.

Church—You don't have to go to a building for the worship of God. Faith is anywhere you see your God and worship him.

Churchgoer—Some people who don't go to church act more Christian than some who attend regularly.

Chute—Some people should remember to open their mouths on the way down, if their parachute doesn't open. All that hot air would provide them with the effects of a hot air balloon.

Cigar—Smoking a cigar doesn't make you a big shot; it's what's between your ears that makes you what you are.

Cigarette—Give these up if you believe your life is too precious to lose.

Cinderella story—It happens everyday, and it can happen to you.

Circle—May your circle of friends include the whole world.

Circular File—Some of the most important papers in life end up here. Either by accident, on purpose, or because at the time there was more room here than on the top of your desk.

Circulation—Learn all you can in life and increase the circulation of your brainpower.

Circumstance—Don't try to understand your surroundings before you accept them, because with acceptance will come understanding.

Circus—Become a kid again and take a kid to the circus. Make one more smile for the world possible.

Citizen—Everyone belongs where their heart desires to be.

City—A first-class city is one that is home to everybody who wants to live there, regardless of race, politics, and religion.

City Hall—A place where hard-earned taxes sometimes go up in smoke for the foolishness of tomorrow.

City Slicker—The opposite of a country hick; when a city slicker and country hick get together, they have a slicking-hicking time.

Civil Rights—Everyone has the right to live as a human being and enjoy life the best they know how.

Civil War—It seems like it is still going on. Only instead of north and south fighting, it's families, neighbors, gangs and if you look at somebody wrong.

Clairvoyance—Just be sure that when you predict the future, you take credit for your wrong predictions as well as your right ones.

Clamp—Keep this handy in your pocket just in case you run into a big mouth.

Clap—When somebody makes you happier than you were before, they deserve your applause.

Clarity—Be clear with your intentions for your beloved, and then maybe marriage for you will truly be a lifelong commitment to your beloved. For better or worse is the reality of life.

Classroom—No matter how big or small your classes in school are, just be sure what goes in your head stays in. Better to learn your lessons now than the harsh one of life later on.

Claustrophobia—If this overtakes you, get help.

Clay—It's beautiful to work with your hands. So if you can work with pottery, do it. The beauty you create will last for the next generation to enjoy.

Clean—Keep the environment this way for the next generation to enjoy and for you to enjoy now.

Clean-cut—Not everyone who appears clean-cut is, so watch out for their bag of tricks when your back is turned.

Cleavage—A boss who hires you only on the merit of being sexy, is a boss who in the long run will not respect you. So in the short run, dress properly and the proper boss will come along and hire you on the merit of being you. Skills between the ears will do you more good and last longer than thrills between the legs.

Clergy—People who are close to God and want to share him with you.

Clerical—Office jobs can be just as hard as those who get their work accomplished. Getting work accomplished requires an effort, no matter what kind of job you have.

Clever—Some people think they are clever, until the IRS audits them, then their silence is golden.

Climate—It is how you feel inside that counts, not the outside forces that affect your life.

Climax—When you reach your highest point, enjoy it, because the slide down is fast.

Climb—When you are not satisfied with ground level, do this.

Clinch—Clinch your safety for you and your family by being aware of everything going on around you. Keep tabs on anything unusual and report any signs of trouble to the police. Too bad, the open door policy of years ago is gone. By this I mean things were so safe you could leave your doors unlocked when you slept.

Clock—Some people wouldn't give anybody the time of day and if they owned all the clocks in the world.

Clodhopper—It doesn't matter how you get where you are going, just so you get there.

Clog dance—Learn this dance and you will bring joy to the hearts of many people.

Clone—Some people you would like to duplicate like President John F. Kennedy. While some other people you wouldn't want to duplicate like Hitler.

Close—They say close only counts in horseshoes, but when you have friends that you are close to, it counts a lot.

Close Call—Remember the situation that caused this, and maybe it won't happen again.

Closet—Every closet should have a light in it. It's almost like a midlife crisis when you get on your hands and knees with a flashlight to find your favorite pair of shoes.

Close-up—Keep your teeth clean, and you won't have to worry about the camera range.

Clothes—Wear what feels good and looks good on you. Don't go by what the next person says.

Cloud—Your life should be like a cloud. Float and pass on by your troubles.

Cloud seeding—Too bad we couldn't get the equivalent of this for some humans and call it brain seeding. Maybe some sense could be put in their heads and some of their foolish ways could be mended.

Cloverleaf—Don't depend upon a four-leaf clover to find success, because people obtain success from hard work, not luck.

Clown—A wonderful profession, because clowns make children and adults laugh, making life a little bit easier for them.

Club—Form one and call it AHFE, (A Home for Everybody).

Clunker—If your car looks and runs like it and arrived on the "Mayflower," maybe you should think about getting another one.

Coach—You can coach a team, but don't forget it's team play that wins games, not coach play.

Coast Guard—They make the coast clear so you can enjoy the shoreline.

Coat—Give one to a needy person in the wintertime if you have an extra one.

Coat of arms—Don't worry about what your coat of arms reads. Stand up for what makes you proud and feel good about yourself.

Coattails—Don't depend on riding somebody's coattails to get into office. If you can't make it on your own, then you stand for very little.

Coax—Don't coax somebody too much to do something they don't want to. Too much coaxing and you destroy the purpose of the thing you wanted them to do.

Cobbler—They make your path smooth, so appreciate them because your feet do.

Cocaine—Too much of this and you won't have to have an airline ticket to fly anywhere, just flap your arms and you can take off and be ready to die.

Cock-and-bull-story—That all males should be macho and tough and that all females should be feminine and soft. Whether you are borsn female or male, be what your heart tells you to be, not what the society dictates you.

Cockfight—This shouldn't be allowed, because there should be peaceful relations even among animals.

Cockroach—For some people this is the only pet they have, and it shouldn't be this way. If you know of people living this way, help them out of this situation. Everybody is entitled to human dignity in order to live a long and healthy life.

Cocktail—Don't drink too many cocktails on an airplane, otherwise you might experience more air pockets than what actually occur.

Cocky—If you get too cocky about anything, you might want to look into a mirror and humble yourself.

Coequal—If people all over the world would treat each other as coequal, everybody could coexist with one another.

Coffee break—Some people work through their break; while some others are on one all day. If everybody did their fair share of work, everybody would get a break and deserve it.

Coffee klatch—Too many of these with dessert, and you will give the states of Texas and Alaska competition for who is the biggest.

Coffin—Contains a dead body, but the soul of the person goes on.

Coin—Did you ever hear about three coins in the fountain? Who can afford the price they charge you to go to Rome and throw coins in the fountain? By the time you pay for the trip, you don't have any coins to toss.

Cold—Good exercise for you, because you move faster in cold weather.

Cold-blooded—If you know somebody cold-blooded, thank God if you're not. People remember the warmth you generate, not the chill.

Cold shoulder—When somebody does this to you, don't stoop to their level, respond with a warm heart.

Cold turkey—Pace yourself when you go cold turkey over something. Take one day at a time, and your success will be the price you worked for.

Collaborate—Do this at work with your fellow workers, and your bread and butter will seem more tasty.

Collar—Remember a collar is for the safety of your pet, not to mistreat him or her with.

Collection—It's sad to think that some churches have to put money collected during a service in a safe place for fear it could be stolen even before church is let out.

Collector—If a bill collector ever comes to your door, be kind to that person. They are only doing their job to earn a living. So meet them all the way, pay your debt, and let your life and their life go on.

College—Not everyone has to go to college to achieve something in life. Just being yourself to the best of your ability equals a master's degree.

College of Cardinals—They pick the next pope in a sea of red; let's hope they don't see red from the strain and long hours that go into this process.

Collision—Be sure you have your seat belts on and maybe a car crash wouldn't be so serious. Be sure if you have small children you have them seated in car seats in the back seat, and be sure you have them fastened in right. It wouldn't hurt to have a car with an air bag.

Cologne—Don't be fooled by fragrances. Your best selling point is your personality, not how you smell.

Color—Show your colors or fly your colors, but remember, when you lose your color, it's time for the doctor.

Colorblind—Jesus died on the cross for everyone. He didn't care what color they were.

Columbus Day—When America was discovered and freedom became something America will stand for forever.

Columnist—Write what you must, but believe what's in your heart.

Coma—All is not lost, because people in a coma administer to the needs of others through their silence. Families are brought closer in a crisis.

Comb—You can comb your hair all you want, but it's the hair that make the hair, not the comb.

Combat fatigue—Some marriages lead to this.

Come—Come to the supper the Lord has prepared for you.

Comeback—Make this a good one, so you have a strong base built to stay in place.

Comedian—Some are in political life; others perform on a stage. You can tell them apart by giving them a lie detector test.

Comic strip—If your level of reading is a comic strip, that means you believe in laughter, and that is one priority in life everybody should have.

Coming-out—Some people who have a coming-out party should stay in.

Commander in Chief—The buck is supposed to stop at his or her desk, but sometimes it gets changed into wooden nickels before they get it, and they can't tell the difference.

Commandment—Some people will misbehave no matter how many commandments there are.

Comment—Talk when it does somebody some good, otherwise don't say anything. Idle chatter never helps anyone.

Commercial—Some people see more sex in a one-minute commercial than they personally experience a whole lifetime.

Commit—Pledge to help others and you will be helping yourself, too.

Common—Nobody is common unless they allow themselves to be.

Common-law marriage—Love is stronger than a piece of paper.

Common sense—More important than having a college degree.

Communication—Silence is not golden when it comes to working for peace.

Communism—Denial of freedom, so be the voice of those who don't have one.

Communist Party—This has gone downhill. Thank God for big miracles.

Community—All the people living in a particular city, who are just as important as people living in a bigger city.

Community center—This is an important part of a community because people who are lonely can come and meet other people who are in the same boat. Also, it is a good place for senior citizens to come and mingle with other senior citizens. The young should be invited to meet their peers. Also, people of all ages can come and meet one another and have some fun.

Community college—It outperforms many bigger colleges and learning a computer will seem like a cakewalk.

Companion—Be one to somebody who doesn't have one.

Company—Some people have company that stays so late they let their dog outside for them in the morning and greet their paperboy on the way out.

Compare—Don't compare anybody or anything, for in the differences of the world is the strength to move forward for the common good of all mankind.

Compass—Know your direction and you will know your course in life.

Compassion—Don't be afraid to show it; some people need it to survive.

Compensate—Make up for the shortcomings of others. If you make the world a better place to live, what difference does it make who does it?

Compete—Enter the race with intentions to win, but even coming in last is better than not being in the race at all.

Complain—Don't complain about anybody or anything unless you can do a better job than the next person.

Complete—Don't start something you don't intend to finish, because no matter what the outcome, you gain experience. So it is well worth your while to complete any project you start.

Complexion—Don't let a bad complexion defeat you. Eat right, exercise right, sleep right, live right, and you will turn out all right.

Complicated—Nothing is complicated if you learn to use the force between your ears. If you don't understand what's going on around you, ask for help. Don't miss anything that will make a difference to your life. Comprehension is the key to your success.

Composer—They write the music that sets our hearts and minds free to enjoy life to its fullest.

Composition—Create compositions that will bring a smile to the world.

Compromise—A settlement is the key to keeping things moving in a solid direction.

Computer—When it starts sassing you, it's time to fight back. Hit it where it hurts, unplug it.

Comrade—Be one to someone who needs a marching buddy to make it to his or her rainbow of tomorrow.

Conceal—Don't conceal too much, because there is too much darkness in this world already.

Concede—Acknowledge defeat, but don't accept it.

Conceit—Think it, but don't show it. It's a positive attitude, not public display, that lends results.

Concentrate—Focus on things that will make life better for you and for others.

Concentration camp—A place where they tried to break the spirit of the people, but they didn't succeed, because the spirit of the people lives on forever.

Concern—Somebody needs this everyday, so give it where needed.

Concert—Go to one and thank God for the talents of others, because the results of long hours of practice went into your ears.

Conclude—Don't decide this until the race is finished.

Concrete—Some people think they have concrete ideas, but they have to watch their footing because their cement is still wet.

Condemn—Let God do the judging, and you take care of your own porch.

Condition—Keep yourself in good condition because the race is won when you have the best to work with.

Condolence—When you offer condolence to somebody, make sure it is from your heart and not just your mouth.

Conduct—May your conduct be the model for others to follow.

Conductor—You are the conductor of your life, so direct it the way you will get the best results.

Confederacy—America was divided during this time, and when you think of the racism in this country, it's still divided.

Confer—Let your heart, soul, and mind confer once in a while, and you will find the results pleasing to all three.

Confession—You will only feel good when you tell all your sins and are sorry for them. The forgiveness and mercy of the Almighty will match your sorrow and then some.

Confetti—Small pieces or streamers of colored paper that are scattered around during the course of festive occasions. I bet people wouldn't throw it around so much if they had to clean it up.

Confidence—You need this in order to avoid being flatter than a pancake.

Confidence game—Don't play this game with anyone. Swindles take away from the quality of life that was meant to be.

Confidential—Avoid secrets. They tend to silence those people who could help you.

Confine—Don't confine your mind, because a "think limit" makes for an unintelligent world.

Confirm—Make sure when you confirm something, your support is strong and you make firmer and strengthen the thing you want to confirm.

Conflict of interest—Tight pantyhose and diarrhea.

Confusion—Don't get bewildered over things that will pass in time.

Congratulations—Give this to anybody who tries, no matter where they finish in a race.

Congregation—People united in the worship of God and working through his hands for the welfare of all.

Congress—If they would pay more attention to the needs of their constituents rather than what the lobbyists want, the problems of today would be a thing of the past.

Congressman, congresswoman—They are not treated fairly because they have to face reelection every two years, whereas the senators face it every six years. Why not be fairer to the people that are closer to their constituents than their counterparts?

Connections—Make sure your connections in life move you towards the goals you laid out for yourself.

Conquer—Conquer your fears and live a life of carefree days.

Conquest—When you make a conquest of something you have been wanting to achieve, celebrate in style but don't overdo. You may want to save some celebration for the next time you achieve a conquest.

Conscience—Develop a good one, and you will do all right in life.

Consent—Only give your consent when your heart is in it.

Consequence—Be willing to pay the price when you step out of bounds but after you have learned your lesson, pick up the pace you had before.

Conservation—Protect the natural resources, not just for future generations, but for you and your generation to enjoy now.

Conservatives—They think they can do no wrong, and when they get caught with their hands in the cookie jar, they say they thought it was their constituents' suggestion box. They also think that on judgment day, God will step aside and let them do the judging of mankind.

Consider—Reflect on the positives of life, not the negatives.

Consistent—Be consistent when you know the price of being right is worth it.

Consolation prize—Sometimes the consolation prize represents the greatest win in the life of the person or persons who receive it.

Console—Make someone less sad and tell them to pass it on.

Conspicuous—Don't be this if it bothers you. Being uncomfortable about attention is not worth the trouble trying to obtain it. Being unnoticed and comfortable is a combination worth living with.

Constant—Give faithful guidance to your children daily. Your efforts will pay off when your children are grown and shaping the world.

Constantine the Great—Constantine was the first Christian Emperor of Rome. Sometimes I wish we had more Christian leaders in the movie industry. Maybe we wouldn't have so much nudity, sex, swearing, and violence in the movies.

Constituent—Write your representative in congress or the President of the United States and give him or her the praise or hell they deserve, because it is through you they either stay in office or leave it.

Constitution—Let's not be afraid to add amendments to the constitution, because it is through freshness that we sustain principle.

Constrict—Don't constrict your mind when wider paths of thinking would serve your purpose more.

Consumer—Be aware of the goods you buy, and you will be a good consumer. Write to companies you think are cheating you and your fellow consumers and tell them what you think.

Contact lens—I think a lot of people think they look better without glasses, but I think some of the cutest people in the world are those who wear glasses. Men do make passes at girls who wear glasses. They do more than that in some cases.

Contempt—Don't despise somebody so much that you forget the meaning of the word love and forgiveness.

Contest—You only lose a contest when you take it to heart instead of doing it for fun.

Continue—Continue the love Jesus showed for mankind by his dying on the cross.

Contortionist—When some couples make love, they end up like this.

Contract—Be sure you understand when you sign, because you may be left holding more than one bag.

Contractor—They build the warmth we enjoy in stormy times.

Contradicted—It's all right to contradict somebody, but make sure it's with your mouth and not your fists.

Contrary—Don't be afraid to be different, because your difference may make the world a better place to live. Also, there is beauty in difference.

Contribution—It is in giving that we receive the greatest joy of all: the knowledge of the love we feel for our fellowman.

Control—Control your temper, and your point will get across in a way more to your liking.

Controversy—Controversy is something that keeps you awake at night. It doesn't do much for those who were able to sleep through it.

Convalescent home—A place where people who think they are going to die are placed so they will have the chance to recover. Wouldn't it be something if they knew this?

Convene—Let's get together and make something worthwhile out of this convention.

Convenient—It's so nice when we can take shortcuts in life, but it's the distance we make that will determine the convenience of our lives.

Convent—A place where people walk around like zombies while people are giving speeches.

Convention—Where people walk around like zombies while people are giving speeches.

Conversation—More conversation between countries would mean less wars, so let's hope for the sake of all mankind that the lips keep moving.

Conversation piece—A birthday suit on an out of shape person.

Conversion—If something gives you peace of mind, you know you made the right change in your life.

Convert—Be good to them; they came over to your side for a good reason.

Convertible—A car doesn't make the person; the person makes the person.

Convict—They can become new again if they let the good that is possible within them surface.

Cook—Learn to do this, and you can fend for yourself if need be. Also, if somebody is sick and can't feed him or herself, you can help them. Men should especially learn to cook then they can give their wives a break once in a while and fix a meal for their families.

Cookbook—The best recipes come from the heart.

Cool—Some people think they are cool; don't let them freeze you out.

Cooperation—It is only through cooperation that we work in a united way for the peace of all mankind.

Coordination—Don't let it bother you if you are clumsy. As you grow older, you will outgrow this then you can look back and have a good laugh over it.

Copartment—Pick a good one, because life is greater when two people work together for the benefit of both.

Cope—Learn to cope because to make it through life, you have to deal with problems.

Copilot—Sometimes giving support is just a great a challenge as doing the flying.

Copycat—Do this of Jesus' life and you will do all right in life.

Copyright—Protect your talent. You worked hard for it.

Cord—Make sure your cord to life is strong. It is the only one you have.

Cordial—Act this way towards people, and they will remember you for ever.

Corduroy—It may not be as fancy as other materials, but the warmth it provides is all that matters.

Core—When you get to the center of your problem, uproot the seeds and don't plant them again.

Cork—Don't let anybody get your cork, because a cork is hard to put back in sometimes.

Corn—A beautiful sight to see is a field of corn that is knee-high by the Fourth of July.

Corner—I know of some people who live in a round house. When their kids to something wrong, for punishment they tell them to go and sit in a corner. Would you believe those kids who are in their thirties and forties, and they are still looking for a corner in the house to sit in?

Cornerstone—Make it a good one; you want it to last for a while.

Corn flakes—One food that anybody can cook.

Cornstarch—Use it the way your mother taught you, and you will please your family at dinnertime.

Corn whiskey—Drink too much of this, and you won't be able to tell your breakfast from your supper.

Coronation—Life is not fair. People who deserve a crown get kicked in the behind, and the people who deserve a good kick get a crown.

Coroner—This is not an easy job, so appreciate the people who do it.

Corporation—Corporations should treat each individual person as important as a group of people.

Correct—Don't let the mistakes in your life get you down. Correcting your mistakes gives you the chance to start over the right way.

Correspondence school—This is the ticket for you if being with people makes your nervous but you still want a college education.

Corrupt—Don't corrupt somebody or something when love can accomplish so much more in your life.

Corsage—A big corsage doesn't make you anymore of a woman than a small one. It's the thought that went into it that should be your size meter.

Corset—The great distributor.

Cosign—Don't cosign something if you don't like the responsibility.

Cosmetic—Something may look nice on the outside, but don't look inside, because you will be disappointed.

Cost of living—If this gets any higher, it is going to give the 747s competition for who can go the highest.

Costume—Some men and women wear one of these year around. You can't see it on the outside but inside you can see it. Men who act like the devil and women who act like a witch have their devil costume and their witch costume on every day of the year on the inside of themselves. Let's hope they change the inside of themselves and instead of a costume they have love for their fellowman and they let it pour forth from their heart to their fellowman everyday of the year.

Costume jewelry—It may be imitation, but it glows just the same.

Cottage—Where you can attain the restful moments needed for your journey through life.

Cottage cheese—Symbol of the millions of people on diets around the world.

Cotton—If you had to pick it, you would appreciate it more.

Couch—Made to put your seat on, not to conceive on.

Cough—Stay home from work if your cough can make a windmill go around.

Council—Don't condemn a council from the sidelines go to a council meeting and give your opinion.

Counsel—Give it if you understand the situation.

Counselor—A good one will give you a good feeling about yourself on just your first visit.

Count—Whether you are counting calories or sheep, don't count yourself out of anything until you take your last breath.

Counterfeit—People who work hard earn the real thing; they don't need to deal with artificial things.

Country—People leave the country to move into towns, but the country never leaves them. Once you have felt the earth, nothing else feels the same.

Country club—Where money talks.

Country folk—They are the heart of America.

Couple—Death can break them up, but it can't destroy the memories. So don't forsake the happiness for fear of the sadness.

Coupon—If products were sold at more reasonable prices, people would be able to afford them without coupons.

Courage—Everybody has courage. Some people have inner courage, which is felt but not seen. Walk a mile in their shoes, and you will realize you just walked a courageous mile.

Courtesy—Be courteous, and you will be remembered for the sunshine you spread.

Courthouse—If heads remain cool, calm, and collected, justice can be accomplished in this building.

Court-martial—A military or naval court of officers appointed by a commander to try persons for offenses under military law. This is a serious matter. One hopes the one on trial gets a fair hearing. Once a decision is made it is hard to take it back. Many a long military career is ruined by this. So the officers doing the judging should take their time and make a thorough decision.

Cover charge—If some restaurants served better food and provided better service, a cover charge wouldn't be needed, because they would have tons of people coming in to eat at their establishment. If they have entertainment it should be for free.

Covered wagon—This could give competition to some of the cars made today.

Cover girl—Don't feel bad if your picture doesn't appear on magazine covers, because you are the cover girl of your life.

Cow—You think the world is dangerous now, wait until cows start flying.

Coward—Don't judge a person by his or her colors, because colors change but so do people.

Cowbell—Ring one when cows start flying and maybe they will come down.

Cowboy, cowgirl—I hope they all go to heaven, so there is a big rodeo in the sky, but with mechanical bulls and other mechanical stuff. Let's be kind to animals once and for all.

Co-worker—Try to get along with your co-workers, because it is only through cooperation with them that products made in the U.S.A. are able to withstand the challenge from the world market.

Crack—Don't crack under pressure, patch the crack up with your will power, and go on from there.

Craft—Learn a hobby, and you won't be bored.

Cranky—Don't pay any attention to cranky people, because then they will realize their crankiness is not doing them any good.

Crawl—Mental illness does this to you. Other people may see you walking, but when you are afflicted with mental illness, you are crawling.

Crazy—Isn't it crazy when you think most people are forced to retire at sixty-five, yet some people older than that run for president of the United States. If somebody can run the country at that age, some of the greatest workers in the world should be allowed to keep working.

Crazy bone—Some people must have more than one and in many places, including their head, when you think of the crimes some of them commit. Nobody in their right mind could be that mean to their fellowman.

Cream—You may not be the cream of the crop. Who cares so long as you keep up with the crop.

Creation—God made a beautiful world. Let's keep it that way.

Credential—Make sure your credentials match your output.

Credit card—You can buy with it, but you can't pay for your bills later with it. So take control of your spending habit before it takes control of you.

Credit union—Nice to have in time of need.

Creek—If you have a creek by your home, take care of it. Leave the future generations something to enjoy and remember you by. Also, while you are preserving it, you can enjoy it.

Crestfallen—Don't be so crestfallen that your posture suffers too. A positive attitude can lift your spirits and help you to become yourself in a positive way again.

Crew cut—No hair in the eyes and not much hair to wash are the advantages of having your hair this way. You can tell your own ghost stories and have the proof on top of your head.

Cricket—Bring out the tea, find the queen, and you're all set to watch a game of cricket.

Crime—I think it's a sin and a shame how some people commit a crime, write a book about it, and then they appear on television and get paid a bundle for that, too.

Crisis—To overcome a crisis you need a level head, so practice clear thinking and you can put it to good use later on.

Crisscross—As you are crisscrossing the country on your vacation, remember the towns you drive through. Just like you are trying to get away from it all, maybe some residents of those towns are traveling, trying to get away from it all, and maybe they are in your town. So appreciate what you left behind.

Criticism—Don't criticize anybody or anything unless you can do better.

Croak—Don't wish somebody you don't like would croak. Let frogs do the croaking and let people do the living.

Crochet—Make something nice for the wearer of your heart.

Crocodile tears—Why do they call them crocodile tears? Has anybody seen a crocodile cry?

Crocus—Spring is here when these appear, so enjoy them while you can. Once gone, it seems spring is gone too for another year much too soon.

Crooked—Don't be this, because if you get caught, you see straight, straight bars, that is.

Crop—Pray for good weather so the farmers of the world can provide for all mankind.

Cross—Jesus died on one, so don't be afraid of one.

Cross-country—Go cross-country when the inner city gets too rough for you.

Cross-country skiing—The pound-shredder and see nature at its best exercise.

Cross-examine—Cross-examine your heart and show more love for your fellowman.

Cross-eyed—Don't worry if you are cross-eyed. Be thankful for what you can see and forget about how you see it.

Cross-dress—Don't condemn people because everybody is different in their own way. Walk a mile in anybody's shoes and I'm sure you will feel different about them. For the better I'm sure.

Crossfire—The tragedy of this is the innocent victims are caught in the middle.

Crow—If people who brag a lot would have to eat more crow, their bragging rights would diminish, and the world would be a quieter and more peaceful place for the rest of us.

Crowd—It's all right to be in a crowd as long as you maintain your individuality and peace.

Crown—Some people you would like to put a crown on their head, while some others you would like to stick it someplace else.

Crucifix—The salvation of mankind through the suffering of one.

Cruel—Don't be cruel, because there is enough pain in the world already.

Crumb—The crumbs on your table may not mean much to you, but to people in need they mean the banquet of their life.

Crusade—Be on a crusade to make life better for all mankind.

Crutch—It's all right to use a crutch when you need one in order to walk, but don't use any other kind of crutch to make it through life. Inner strength is the greatest supporter you'll ever need in your lifetime.

Cry—Don't be ashamed to cry, whether in public or in private. Tears were meant for the outside of the face, not the inside. Just don't go to the extreme and become a crybaby. Do your share in life; don't bellyache your way through it.

Crystal—The pride of glass. Let your life be the pride of the world.

Crystal ball—A future depended on a crystal ball is one that is fragile and breakable. Only you can provide yourself with a strong and enduring future.

Cub scout—A wonderful training ground to teach young boys how to make the world a better place for all mankind.

Cuckoo clock—Some people are like a cuckoo clock, the only thing you don't see is the bird come out of their head. Once in a while you hear the cuckoo sound coming out of their mouth.

Cuddle—Cuddle only those people who want to be cuddled.

Cue—Know your cue to life, and green will be your signal to go on with your life.

Culottes—Wear them if you feel comfortable in them than a regular skirt. Style should be your own choice when it comes to your free spirit and well-being.

Cultivate—Develop your mind so you can harvest a good crop of ideas in years to come.

Culture—What you are is your culture, so don't think you have to learn something new to be accepted into high society. Accept yourself and be your own high society.

Cup—If your cup runs over, pour the spillover into the cup of another person who needs it.

Cupid—Don't play cupid if you can't keep your own true love contented.

Cure-all—For the soul, it's confession; for the body, it's taking yucky medicine when the body hurts.

Curfew—Don't give your children hell for missing a curfew, just thank God they're home. There is not such thing as a curfew to the parents of missing children.

Curious—Your way to knowledge is through this.

Current—Know what is current, so that you can do your part to shape the world of tomorrow.

Curse—Don't curse what can't be changed. Make up your mind to do better the next time.

Curtain—A curtain was meant to provide, not divide.

Curtain call—Just because you're not applauded at work doesn't mean your coworkers don't appreciate you. Maybe there is silent applause going on for you everyday.

Curve—Be careful of the curves in life, because they can lead to the ditches of tomorrow.

Cushy—Your job may not be cushy, but at least you've earned your keep.

Custom—Tradition is okay as long as it doesn't impede the development of new customs that would mean a better future for those involved.

Customer—If you want the floor in your place of business to suffer from the wear and tear of the pitter-patter of your customers' feet, keep your store socked with products built to their satisfaction.

Cut—When you throw junk mail away, be sure you cut out your name and address into tiny pieces. That way nobody can get your name and address and use it for whatever purpose they have in mind.

Cute—Looking cute deserves applause; acting cute deserves a kick in the behind.

Cut glass—This may be expensive, but water is more precious.

Cutler—They provide the tools for the food for thought.

Cutup—Be careful your practical jokes don't lead to an uppercut from an impractical person.

Cycle—They say life is an endless cycle, but don't fear it. Live it to the best of your ability and see your life become a cycle to remember.

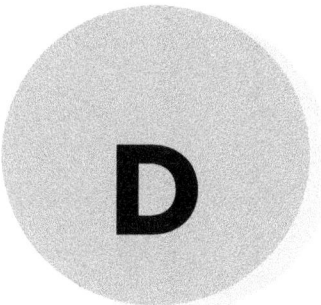

Daffodil—A pretty flower that turns yellow into color of beauty and strength, not the weakness mentioned so often of it.

Dairy—When you eat a dairy product, remember the work that went into it, and maybe you will appreciate and help the family farms.

Dalmatian—Symbol of the courage of the fire fighters of America.

Damage—Assess the damage, then surround yourself with the possibilities.

Dampen—Don't depress anybody, because we need all the lively people we can get to establish a more livable world.

Dance—Everybody can dance, just move your feet in whatever direction you want and you are dancing no matter what anybody says.

Dandruff—Don't worry if you have dandruff. Nowadays white is dignified.

Danger—Take care of yourself and your family. Be alert of people and things around you. This way you won't be caught off guard if danger is in your future. If you are prepared, danger can't harm you and your family.

Dare—Dare to be brave and you will be.

Daredevil—Be bold, but don't be lost to your family forever because of one foolish act.

Dark—Don't be afraid of the dark, because fear doesn't. It come from darkness. It comes from the inside of you, and you can control it if you want to.

Dark Ages—Don't step back in time, move ahead, and walk new steps everyday of your life.

Dark horse—Sometimes the dark horses are the best winners in the world.

Dash—Years ago it was dashing through the snow in a one-horse open sleigh; nowadays it's skidding across the road in a lemon of a car.

Dashboard—It's better to have an air bag blow up in your face than to have the dashboard blues after an accident.

Day—Taking one day at a time is the greatest survival tip in the world. Also, every day on the calendar should be a happy one for you, because it is one more day the Lord has made, so rejoice and be glad in it.

Daydream—Don't daydream unless your dreams are the path to the reality of your success.

Dazzle—Don't be so overwhelmed by something that you can't tell what is reality and what is fantasy.

Deadbeat—Don't be this, because your energy is needed for a better world.

Dead-end—Don't let the dead-ends of life stop you. Find the detours that will lead you in grand style.

Dead letter—No letter is dead, because of the emotion and love that went into the writing of the contents.

Dead Sea—Don't let your mind become this. Think in terms of a live wire.

Dean—To be dean of a college means you have to stay on the job even when it gas tough and do the job you were appointed to.

Dear—Be sure the one you call dear is the one you are married to. Say dear too much in the wrong direction and it may lead to one dear too many.

Death—When people die, they don't go to their destiny alone. Your love for them goes with them, and they leave behind their love for generations to enjoy forever.

Debate—Know your facts before you debate.

Debt—Don't charge so much that you pay out more in interest than the interest you earn on your saving account.

Debut—Make your debut in life a good one, so people remember you as good Charlie Brown instead of Big Bad John.

Decay—Don't let your teeth get so bad that a football team could kick a field goal through them.

December—The month of Christmas and joy. It should be a month long birthday celebration in honor of Jesus.

Decent—Fight for this in life, and you will have done your part for mankind.

Decide—To make up one's mind is a major responsibility. So don't shirk your responsibility, because your decision making power is the greatest link to being independent in life.

Deck hand—It sounds like a secondary job, but it isn't. People who take a cruise will remember this person more than the captain. A good impression by a deck hand brings in more tourist trade for a cruise company than anybody or anything else.

Declaration of Independence—The adoption of this in 1776 assured America of having no kings and queens, just politicians galore.

Decoy—Be careful of Satan. He is the greatest decoy of them all.

Dedicate—Be dedicated to the one you love.

Deep—Have a deep love for your country, your fellowman, and nature, and you will do all right in life.

Deer—I prefer to see deer loose and running wild rather than stiff and tied down on a car going fifty-five miles an hour or more down the highway.

Deface—Don't deface the joy of others.

Defeats—Our of your defeats can come some of your greatest victories.

Defect—When you sin, you have a defect on your soul. Only a good confession will rid your soul of it. So remember that when you sin, especially if it's a major sin. It takes a real good confession to wash away a major sin, otherwise if you don't confess it and die, you won't make it to Heaven.

Defend—Thanks to the millions of men and women who defended our country in war in order for the rest of us to enjoy our freedom in America.

Defendant—Don't prejudge anybody. The appeals process can lay aside a verdict on the slightest indiscretion. So all sides hush until the facts are in.

Defense spending—It's okay to spend on defense as long as you don't forget about the needy, otherwise there won't be anybody left to defend.

Defrost—The mind needs a good defrosting once in a while. So don't be afraid to flush some old ideas out and think up some new ideas in.

Degrade—It's much better to upgrade than to degrade.

Delight—Delight those around you and hope they pass it on. A happy world is the key to a successful world.

Deliver—Don't tell jokes if you can't deliver the punch lines the way they should be told.

Delivery—Deliver your heart when your love is needed in a special way.

Demand—Don't make demands on people that even you can't fulfill.

Demolish—Demolish sin and replace it with the goodness of your heart.

Demonstrate—Show your willingness to work with other people, because it is only through cooperation that success is achieved.

Dentist—Don't be afraid of the dentist, because if you don't go to one, you may eventually see your teeth floating around in a water-filled glass at night.

Denture—If your dentures keep clicking after you take them out of your mouth, you know you talk too much.

Deodorant—Better for your deodorant to give out than for you to give up.

Depend—Be someone people can count on, and you will be a more responsible person.

Deposit—Make enough deposits so that your golden age really will be golden.

Depression—Don't allow yourself to lie in the gutter too long, otherwise you will become part of the gutter.

Deprive—Where love is deprived, hate isn't far behind. Don't give hate a leg to stand on. Your heart's chief product is love, so use it.

Depth—It isn't how much love you show for somebody in life that counts, but the quality of love you show somebody.

Derelict—Don't condemn them unless you have walked in their shoes for a while.

Desert—Don't knock the wasteland. After all, there's water in the cactus and there's no lawn to cut.

Dessert—Don't eat too much of this, because instead of coming to the table to eat, you will be the table.

Destiny—Lead a good life and when you die your destiny will be Heaven.

Destitute—Help reverse this situation in the world if you can.

Destitute—Help reverse this situation in the world if you can.

Destroy—It's better to build than to destroy.

Detection—A detective usually is a member of a police force. They are important in the solving of crime. They are good at solving old cases. Cases which are ten or fifteen years old. So they deserve our applause.

Determine—Decide how much effort you want to put into something before you start doing it. If it isn't enough, don't start it because efforts not spent in a worthwhile manner are efforts better spent not at all.

Develop—See to it your children have the proper education, because the proper development of a child's mind means a brighter future for the world.

Devil—For some people life is like being between the devil and the deep blue sea. For others it's like sleeping between their wife and their mother-in-law, and still others it's like listening to a person with a lot of hot air between the ears.

Devil's food cake—Whether it's devil's food cake, deviled ham, or deviled eggs, don't blame it on the devil if you eat too much. Take control of yourself and take responsibility for your own actions.

Devour—Don't eat up everything in sight, because your sight may be deceiving you and you may become a devourer of unhealthy substances.

Diabetics—They have a hard road to go, because most of us like sweets and are able to eat them.

Dial—Make sure you dial the right number when you use the telephone, because it may be hard for the other party to get to the phone.

Diamonds—The diamonds people wear are not as great as the diamond you can have within: Jesus Christ.

Diamond anniversary—Any couple that stays married this long deserves a celebration on the grandest scale. In this age of divorce, it's nice to see where love can make all the difference in the world.

Diaper—Years ago babies had to be changed, and their diapers had to be washed. Now there are disposable diapers. In years to come there will be a diaper that changes itself.

Diary—If you are afraid for somebody to see your diary then don't write anything in it that would offend anybody.

Dice—Don't play with these too much, because your numbers won't always come up. If this happens too much, you won't be able to provide for your family. A gambler's delight sometimes becomes a family's nightmare.

Dictator—They have too much hot air coming out of their mouth and a lot of air space between the ears.

Dictionary—Anybody can write a book. A book is just the dictionary with the words all mixed up and some repeated.

Diet—In America, a lot of people diet to be thin. If we lived in Africa, we wouldn't have to worry about that.

Difference—Be the difference to those people who need help in life.

Difficulty—When you overcome a difficult task, the joy is greater than overcoming a lesser one.

Digestion—Eat properly and your stomach will feel like a merry-go-round ride instead of a roller coaster.

Dignitary—Usually a dignitary has a big car to ride in and the head to match, if you know what I mean. Give me a dignitary who will ride in a Volkswagen and treat people as special in their own way, and you will have a dignitary who deserves your respect.

Dike—Be sure the flooding of love from your heart isn't prevented by a dike within yourself.

Dime—It was nice years ago when you could buy a cup of coffee for a dime. Now all you can get for a dime is the amount you can fill an eyedropper with.

Dinner jacket—I'm sure a lot of people who are starving don't care what they wear for dinner, just so they have a dinner to eat.

Dinosaur—If dinosaurs were alive today, people would have to watch out for, "Beware of Dinosaur" signs instead of, "Beware of Dog" signs.

Diploma—If you are an adult of any age and you don't have your high school diploma, don't fuss. You can go to a special school and earn it. You are never too old to go back to school.

Diplomat—A dangerous job because you can be taken hostage. Even a country considered safe, this could happen. So appreciate a diplomat.

Direction—Know the direction of your life. When you change your mind about something, you will know the way home again.

Director's chair—Too much direction from the occupant of this chair, and a movie can lose the freshness of acting on instinct from the actors and the lens of the camera picking it up.

Dirt cheap—Anything that is made or paid for by the sweat of the brow isn't dirt-cheap.

Dirty campaign—Come election time there are dirty campaigns run by some politicians. No wonder the world seems wicked sometimes. Some politicians don't set very good examples for the youth of America to follow.

Disarm—Wouldn't it be nice if all countries would disarm? It's frightening to think the fate of millions is in the hands of a few. Believe in God, and it will be in His hands alone.

Disaster—If a tornado or a hurricane or some other disaster hits a town, people from surrounding communities should pitch in and help clean it up. You never can tell when you might need the same help in the future.

Disciple—Be a follower of Jesus. You can't go wrong. He died on the cross for you.

Discipline—It's all right to be strict, but don't discipline your children out of your home and into the street.

Disc jockey—Some do more talking than playing of music. A good one will let the music do the talking.

Discount—Just remember something on discount may be on its last leg, in other words, on its way out as a style.

Discovery Day—The day Columbus discovered America. You should discover yourself as a human being that day and stand up and be a part of the human race and America.

Disease—Let's work together to wipe it out.

Disguise—Don't wear a disguise too often, unless you want people to think of Halloween every time they see you.

Dishes—So what if you don't have China to eat off. Just be thankful you have something to eat.

Dishwasher—Don't feel bad if you don't have a dishwasher and you have to wash dishes by hand. Some people with arthritis wish they could wash dishes by hand.

Dislike—Don't dislike too many people; you never can tell when you will need somebody's help in your time of need.

Dismiss—Don't send away anybody or anything that can't be replaced.

Disobey—Disobey only when the result will be good conquering evil.

Dispatcher—An important job because you are keeping people on time, as you send out trains, buses, trucks or cars with promptness and speed according to a schedule.

Display—Display your best talents when you want to get ahead in life. It is only when we do our best that we get the best results.

Disrobe—Disrobe only if you are alone or with your husband. If you are single in front of your mother and sisters is okay. Don't do it in front of your boyfriend. Especially don't do it in front of a man you are living with but not married to. It's important today to do what is right. There is enough bad in this world already. Don't contribute to it. The same conditions go for men with members of the opposite sex.

Distance—Shorten the distance between the people you love by sending a card or telephoning them.

Distinguish—Distinguish the name you carry, and you will know that life is what you are willing to work for. The end results will be dreams that come true.

Disturb—Don't bother anybody unless some good will come out of it.

Ditch—Don't knock people who dig ditches. After all, some of them are building the future home for many of us.

Dive bomber—Let's hope these don't have to be used for anything anymore.

Divide—Don't divide people into either men or women. We are all human beings, no matter what sex we are. Some are weak and some are strong, but all are children of God.

Divulge—Don't divulge anything that will hurt somebody just for the sake of your own pleasure. The price for self-satisfaction shouldn't be based on pain for somebody else.

Do—Try to do what is right for you, and I'm sure it will be right for everybody else, too.

Dock—If your ship hasn't come in yet, maybe you are looking for the wrong kind of ship. Maybe you should be looking for a canoe instead of a yacht.

Doctor—A good one is worth a million dollars and then some.

Dogcatcher—Don't blame dog catchers for rounding up dogs. After all, in many cases they are rounding them up because their owners let them run loose.

Dog days—When you can tar your driveway with your rubber tree plant.

Dog-eat-dog—Do your part to replace a dog-eat-dog society with a people-help-people society.

Dogfight—People who arrange illegal, organized fight between dogs, for spectator entertainment and betting should be put in jail. It is bad enough when dogs on the street fight.

Doghouse—Stick yourself in a real doghouse outside during the wintertime, and you will see how some animals have to live. In the summertime when it is real hot it can be worse especially if the dog is outside in a doghouse with no water to drink.

Dolphin—They are beautiful animals to see perform. If you can go to a place and get in the water and touch them, that is a wonderful experience.

Dome—Nice to have in bad weather, but when the sun shines, open up your heart and let it shine in.

Domestic—If you can do your own work, do it. The time may come soon enough when somebody has to do it for you.

Dominate—Don't dominate anybody. Everybody has the right to be himself or herself.

Donkey—Slow, but at least you don't have to change the oil.

Doomsday—When your mother-in-law wants to move in with you in order to get closer to you.

Doors—Keep your doors locked at all times. People should be welcome in your home, but on your terms, not theirs.

Doorman—Be nice and cheerful to them because they open the door for everybody, no matter what their occupation and skin color is.

Dope—It's bad enough to have to take medicine when you are sick; that some people take drugs and get a kick out of it doesn't make sense. Life is confusing enough sometimes without taking drugs to add to the confusion.

Dormant—Don't become so lazy that people can't tell the difference between you and a doormat.

Double-cross—Don't double-cross anybody, unless making promises doesn't mean anything to you. Shame on you if it doesn't.

Double feature—You almost need a blindfold and earplugs when you see one movie nowadays, let alone two.

Doubt—Don't doubt anything until you see the proof of the pudding, then make up your mind whether your appetite has been satisfied or not.

Dough—I like to eat the dough right out of the bowl before anything is made out of it.

Dove—A white dove will always be the symbol of peace to me.

Down—Don't get discouraged when you are down, because the next step is up.

Downhearted—Don't be downhearted when the upbeat of your heart sounds so much better.

Down-to-earth—It's okay to be down-to-earth, but be sure you keep some of the city lights on.

Draft—Let people go into service on their own, and they will march to their own tune, not somebody else's

Drag—If you want to dress drag in public, you better remember the right place to go when you have to go to the bathroom.

Dragged—If you feel like something the cat dragged in, don't feel bad. At least you were dragged in; look at the people who are left outside in the cold.

Drain—If something is draining you, plug it up with the strength you have within.

Drama—The real drama is in the world, not on a stage or a screen.

Draw—Anybody can draw. If you know what the picture is, who cares if nobody else does.

Drawbridge—If the drawbridge of your life is raised, learn to pole vault.

Drawers—Don't put your hands in anybody else's drawers, unless you are married to the owner of the drawers.

Drawing card—You are the only drawing card when it comes to representing yourself, so do a good job.

Dread—If you dread doing something that has to be done, the sooner you do it, the better off you'll be.

Dream—In life, don't let anyone make fun of your dreams. In life, don't let anyone stop you from dreaming your dreams. In life, don't let anyone stop you from achieving your dreams, because you want your dreams to come true. After all, dreams are free, so the sky is the limit.

Drift—It's okay to drift from shore, but don't stay away so long that you don't recognize it when you return.

Drive—Drive safe so the joy of your family seeing you reach home can be experienced by the families of those drivers you met on the highway, too.

Drive-in—Where people used to make out; now you are lucky if there is a drive-in left.

Driveway—Don't be too slow in life, like the person who was leaving for work and saw his neighbor backing out of his driveway. When he returned home from work at the end of the day, his neighbor was still backing out of his driveway.

Drop—A drop in the bucket is better than nothing at all.

Drought—Perseverance on the farm can outlast anything and keep you smiling even when there are cracks around your foundation.

Drug raid—It's not so funny when a drug raid team gives a wake-up call to the wrong address.

Drum—It's okay to beat your own drum, but don't beat it so loud that even your own ears can't stand the noise. After all you are marching to your own drumbeat and not someone else's. So let your beat be music to your ears.

Duchess, Duke—You don't have to marry a Duke or a Duchess to be a special person. You have a specialty nobody can duplicate: yourself.

Duck soup—Life may be duck soup today, but be prepared, for tomorrow it may be like nailing Jell-O to a wall.

Dude ranch—Nice place to get a feel of the west.

Due—Pay what you owe anybody and go home with a clear conscience.

Duel—I'm glad this era is gone. If a person is a bad shot, the wrong person could get shot, like an onlooker, which could turn him or her into nolooker.

Dull—If something is dull, be like a rainbow and brighten it up.

Dumb—Nobody is dumb. Everybody has a different level of intelligence.

Dump—Don't dump your troubles on anybody else, because when you handle your own troubles, you grow as a person.

Dust—When the weeds start growing on top of your refrigerator, it's time to dust.

Dust bowl—A football game played inside a dusty house.

Dutch treat—Good idea, because your idea to treat someone else may be a seven-course meal at an expensive French restaurant in the eyes of the person you want to treat.

Duty—It's your duty to conduct yourself in a way that your parents will be proud to call you their own.

Dwarf—Most of them are giants in the way they conduct themselves in the world. They have turned their scars into stars.

Dwindle—People decline as human beings when they mistreat others.

Dying—Dying is nothing to be scared of, because it is a part of life and indicates a new direction.

Dynamic—Use all the energy you have to make it a better world for everyone and everything.

Dynasty—Don't forget if your dynasty ever falls: a family that picks up the pieces together, stays together.

Eager—Be eager to get up and go in the morning, and you won't be stopped by any potential pitfalls.

Eagle—Be like an eagle and soar up in the sky, and you won't miss the pleasure of reaching the top.

Ear—Hear only what you want, but don't blame anybody else but yourself for what you miss.

Early bird—The early bird catches the worm, but not too early, because the person who rises early in the morning needs strength to complete his or her tasks.

Earn—Earn as much as you can, but don't be jealous of somebody else making more. It isn't how much you make that counts, it's what you do with your money after you earn it.

Earsplitting—Don't play anything too loud that it hurts the ears of other people especially senior citizens.

Earth—Take care of it so that some space is left for the next generation to enjoy.

Earthquake—You need to use the strength from inside you if you ever experience one of these, in order to survive.

Ease—Ease the pain of others through your willingness to accept some of it yourself.

Easel—Ease your struggle in life by painting. Creativity is life's way of saying, "I'm not so bad." Express yourself and see for yourself.

Easter—You can rise from the dead like Jesus did, and with a soul filled with grace, you can become part of eternal life.

Easy—Make life easier for somebody, and the reward for you will be the joy you see on their face.

Eat—Eat all you want, but don't blame anybody but yourself when you have to buy clothes from Omar the Tentmaker.

Eavesdrop—Just be sure when you eavesdrop you don't give yourself away by perking up your ears too much.

Eccentric—Some people may seem strange to you, but maybe they have something you desire: a peace of mind.

Echo—May all the echoes in your life repeat what you want to hear.

Economy—Let's hope for the day when everybody has the same standard of living and hunger is vanished forever.

Ecstatic—Show great delight when something good happens to someone else, because we are all trying to make it through the night.

Edelweiss—This song is worth listening to. It will bring a smile to your heart.

Edge—The advantage can be yours if you work hard and keep a cool head. But if you find yourself working too hard, edit out some work time and take some time out for some leisure time.

Editor in chief—Be sure the paper you edit is one you would want to come home to.

Education—You need it, so learn and use it everyday of your life.

Efficient—Be efficient when you are assigned something, and you will see people trusting you. An efficient person can handle responsibility.

Effort—Use your energy wisely, because your achievement will show how wisely you used it.

Egg—Get more baskets and spread your eggs around.

Eggnog—Drink one too many of these with an alcoholic liquor added such as rum or brandy and you won't be able to tell yesterday, today and tomorrow apart.

Elapse—Don't let time pass without taking notice, because each moment is precious.

Elastic—Be flexible and show your courage for change.

Elbow grease—If elbow grease doesn't do the job maybe saying the Lord's prayer will.

Elbowroom—Freedom means everybody having enough elbowroom to do his or her own thing. America is the elbowroom capital of the world.

Elderly—Take care of them; they have provided your future.

Elect—No matter who gets elected to an office, they are still probably considered the worst human being alive according to the losing side.

Election—Elections should be held every one hundred years. That way a person wouldn't have to worry so much about suffocating from all the hot air.

Electoral college—I think presidents should be elected by the popular vote, not the electoral college. After all, we are all citizens of the United States, not just the people who live in the states with the most electoral votes.

Electric chair—You would think this would deter some people from committing a murder, but it isn't hot enough to stop them.

Electric guitar—If you play well enough, you can provide your own juice without the electricity.

Electricity—If your lights go out, light a candle and remember the warmth. Let the darkness be a remembrance of warmth, not coldness.

Elements—If you use the right elements daily, your progress in life will be daily, too.

Elephants—Elephants may look clumsy and overweight, but look at the joy they have brought to millions.

Elevators—I don't like elevators, but I suppose we need them to keep up with the skyscrapers of today. To me though, they are like closets on the move.

Eleventh hour—Don't wait until the eleventh hour to get to know God. Get to know him now on a regular basis. Your salvation depends on it.

Eliminate—I hope when you delete something, you have a good recall, in case you need it again later on.

Elite—Don't worry if you aren't part of an elite group, because you know what your best is. Your best may be better than the elite's best.

Elope—People used to use a ladder to elope; now they use an elevator.

Embargo—Don't let anybody or anything prohibit you from being your complete self. Nobody can be you better than you can.

Embark—Every day is a journey you take. Offer up everything you do for the glory of God, and he will smooth your road for a safe journey.

Embassy—God bless those who serve overseas, because they are serving us so we can have freedom in America.

Embrace—Embrace your fellowman and hope countries do the same to each other and exist in peace.

Emerald—A beautiful stone, but be sure it is the color of the stone you like and not the color of envy you possess for somebody who has an emerald.

Emergency—Don't freak out when there is an unforeseen situation that requires immediate action. Stay cool, calm, and collected, and you will see the results you want.

Emergency room—Appreciate people who work in a hospital emergency room. They never know what condition the patients will be in when they are brought in. In some severe car accidents, they may be dealing with limb reattachments and heaven knows what. If a patient dies, they have to have the courage to tell the relatives. So give them a pat on the back for a job well done.

Emigration—I wish everybody's homeland was home to them and not a reign of terror, causing them to flee their homeland.

Emotions—They keep you going. Just keep them on an even keel, and you will do all right.

Empire State Building—Some people come at you like the empire state building but don't let that bother you. Look what David did to Goliath.

Employment—Cleaning toilets everyday is just as important a job as being the president of a company. Don't judge people by their jobs. Appreciate them for what they are as human beings.

Empty—Don't live life without meaning. Fill your life with activities that will put feeling into your life. God helps those who help themselves.

Empty-headed—Don't feel bad if people think you are empty-headed. Some of these so-called full-headed or computer heads could have sunk the Titanic. They are as cold as an iceberg.

Emulates—Watch whom your child emulates. A child imitating the wrong person could break a father's and mother's heart.

Enchantment—Don't be so charmed by somebody or something that you can't tell the difference between reality and fiction.

Encouragement—Give courage to those who need it in order to survive.

Encyclopedia—Read it and learn about new avenues of life.

End—An end has a beginning, and a beginning has an end. They complement each other.

Endanger—Don't endanger anybody's life, even for revenge. Joy based on the suffering of somebody else is a sick joy that shouldn't see the light of day.

End man—The person at the end of a line or row, which isn't a bad position to be in. The line has to stop somewhere. Some of your best people in the world are stoppers.

Endorsement—Give your support to ideas that mean betterment for all mankind.

Endurance—If you have a high endurance rate, help those who don't.

Enemy—Everybody is on one ship: the earth. So try and get along with everyone, because one more candle lit to help you get through the night is well worth the effort.

Energy—Don't overdo and use up all your energy. Save some for a rainy day.

Engaged—Don't become engaged unless your heart is in it.

English Channel—Some people can swim the English Channel. Some people can swim down a river. Some people can swim across a lake, but people in wheelchairs guided by their will power are the greatest swimmers of them all.

Enhance—Improve the surroundings around you for a more beautiful world.

Enjoy—Enjoy life, for laughing is the key to breaking up a sad world.

Enlightener—Be one and help delete ignorance from the world.

Enlist—These are brave souls, those who enlist for service in the armed forces. They are defending the freedom we enjoy in America. So if you see one, shake his or her hand and say thank you.

Enough—Make your goal in life to see to it that everybody has enough food to eat in your area and hope it spreads.

Enroll—Enroll yourself in your mind and take all the credits you can, and you will graduate to your highest potential.

Entertainer—Anybody can be an entertainer. If you make people laugh, you are one.

Enthusiasm—Don't hide it if you want to inspire, because an eager mind is a road people will want to follow.

Entrance—May the doorway to your house be the peace people who enter are looking for.

Entrust—Entrust your love to people who will appreciate it and care for it.

Envelope—Before you seal an envelope, make sure you are satisfied with the contents, because once an envelope is sealed and on its way, you are no longer in control of it.

Environment—Protect the environment, because if you don't, the air you breathe won't be worth taking in.

Envy—Don't desire anybody else's advantages, because if you take your own qualities into account and build on them, you should do all right.

Epilepsy—This illness throws an element of uncertainty into the lives of the people it affects, but they go on with their lives with one certain thought: they have no choice but to fight on. Hats off to them.

Equal—Everybody is born equal, but some people forget the meaning of it sometimes.

Equator—Where it is too hot to trot.

Equipment—Be sure you have the right equipment to hook the big catch in life. The equipment you need is knowledge for the catch known as career goals. The more you learn, the more your dreams come true.

Erase—Erase bad memories from your mind and store the good ones for future reference.

Erect—Build up in your mind a foundation for positive thinking and do wonders for the world.

Error—An error is good practice for the next time you do the same chore again, so it won't be repeated.

Escalator—I don't know why some people take an escalator because they are in such a hurry. They don't wait for steps to move them. They walk up or down the escalator, just like the stairs. They should use the stairs and let the people who want to relax for a few moments ride the escalator.

Escape—Escape the tension in your life by taking a trip. But don't take your same self along. You won't enjoy your vacation if your attitude doesn't change. Release of self is the only way you will enjoy yourself.

Escort—Don't be reluctant to double date on your first date if your parents want you to. Safety in numbers is better than being in the fast lane and uncontrollable.

Eskimos—They taught the whole world how to live with just the bare necessities.

Essential—Knowing who you are, where you are now, and where you want to go is a must.

Establish—Pattern your life so people can look up to you as an example to be followed.

Establishment—Everybody the talks against the establishment, but nobody claims to be the establishment. So who in the hell are they talking about?

Estimate—Find out how much practice it takes for you to live up to your highest potential.

Eternity—Be good and you can have this.

Ethics—Everybody should practice good ethics.

Etiquette—Never mind etiquette. Do what's in your heart.

Eucharist—Receive it daily. It is only through receiving the body of Christ that we realize our love for Him and his love for us.

Euthanasia—Before you end somebody's life, think whose pain you are considering. Is it the suffering your loved one is going through, or is it the pain you are going through from watching him or her suffer? God never gives anybody more pain than they can handle. God loves those who are suffering and will take care of them.

Evangelist—They spread the word and see the happiness it can bring to the people who hear it.

Even—We all start out this way, but along the way things aren't distributed the way they should be. So hand onto your hat as you march on.

Evening gown—It isn't the gown that makes the person. So don't worry if you don't have a thing to wear to a social event. The beauty from within will show you off more than a fancy gown.

Evergreen—Plant one and add to the beauty of nature.

Everywhere—God is everywhere, so make him proud.

Evil—Avoid this as much as possible. Why fight temptation when you don't have to?

Examine—Examine your conscience, and if you don't like what you see, it's time to clean house.

Example—Set a good example for the rest of the world to follow.

Excel—Find out what you are good at and give it all you can.

Exchange—Get in the habit of exchanging friendly greetings with people and you will be the cheerer-upper they need.

Excite—Get excited about things that will make for a better world.

Excursion—Take a trip around your heart and see if you are putting out all the love you are capable.

Excuses—Don't make excuses for mistakes you know you made. It is a waste of time. Admit your mistakes and go on from there.

Executive—Don't feel bad if you are nor an executive, in your own office. Some executives can play marbles at noontime and they don't have to go to a store to buy them.

Executive Mansion—A place where you see what your taxes bought, like furniture, China, paintings, etc.

Exist—With mental illness you just exist. Overcome it and live again.

Expel—Expel thoughts from your mind that upset you.

Experience—The only experience gained is from presence on the job. Never say to a person that she or he doesn't have any experience needed for the job. How can they get any if you don't hire them?

Expert—It isn't how much you know that makes you an expert. It's how you apply what you know that counts.

Explain—Don't try to explain your existence. God put you here for a reason and your existence is justified.

Explore—Explore your mind; you might find some areas you never knew existed.

Explorer—The brave who discover the knowledge for all mankind to benefit from.

Express—Express yourself when it will make a difference in your life for the betterment of you and your loved ones.

Expressway—Don't drive so fast that you take the concrete with you.

Extend—Stretch your hand out to a person in need.

Eye—Take care of your eyes, for they are the sight of your future.

Eye bank—Thank God for this, because with it the light at the end of the tunnel is seen bigger and brighter by many a person.

Eye opener—To streak in below zero weather.

Eye shadow—When a woman uses too much of this, it looks like eye giant.

Face—It's all right to take care of your face, but don't forget about your heart, soul, and mind, too.

Fact—The facts of life should be explained to a child when he or she asks about it. We gain nothing from ignorance. Everything is gained from knowledge.

Fail—You only fail when you don't go on after making a mistake.

Fair—Life doesn't seem fair sometimes, but who said it was going to be? I guess nobody, but then one can at least hope and pray it will be for everybody someday. Until then, let's hope everybody has the strength to survive.

Faith—Everybody who drives a car has faith. They believe when they put on the brakes, the car will stop.

Faith healer—It's all right to treat disease with prayer as long as the God-invented backup known as a doctor is present in case of prayer failure.

Fall—It was meant for the leaves to fall, not you.

Fall guy—Sometimes the fall guy has more potential in his little finger than your so-called Mr. Right.

False alarm—Better to cry wolf than be unprepared and become a dead duck.

False arrest—False arrest sometimes leads to imprisonment, which is terrible, because look at all the criminals who deserve prison and are running around on the street.

Falsify—Don't falsify anybody's hope, because hope is the only means of existence some people have.

Fame—Don't be jealous of well-known people, because everything comes out in the wash. In a hundred years, they will be stiffer than all get-out.

Family—The greatest structure in life, so appreciate your family if you have one. If you don't, then let the world be your family. I'm sure there are people out there willing to embrace you in theirs.

Family Tree—Be yourself and don't worry about what the other branches are like. As long as the trunk is strong, the branches can do their own thing and have a firm base to return to.

Famine—Did you hear the joke about the fat man who met a thin man? The fat man said to the thin man, "You look like you were in a famine." The thin man replied, "You look like you caused it."

Fancy—Fancy doesn't count when it comes to real value. You don't have to put up a front for anything worth-while.

Far—Shorten the distance between you and a loved one. Use the telephone.

Farmer—A person who grows food for thought. Without food you can't think, because you wouldn't have any strength to. So appreciate the farmers of the world.

Farmhand—With their hard work, they are helping to save the family farm.

Fashion Plate—A fashion plate is okay as long as you know where the fashion ends and the person begins.

Fear—If you are afraid of something, ask yourself why and then work to overcome it.

Feather—Most people you can tickle with a feather, but a few it takes a whole ostrich before you can get a laugh out of them.

Fee—The commission that some people get as a sales representative or an agent for services rendered is highway robbery.

Feedback—Pay attention to the feedback in your life. It is the one chance you have to improve your life and to have the best outcome.

Feeling—Something that comes with the turf of being a human being.

Fence—Make sure you put up a fence on your property, not in your mind.

Fence Sitter—It's all right to take a position of neutrality on issues as long as your behind doesn't get too many splinters from the fence.

Ferris Wheel—Life is like a ferris wheel; you want to get to the top, but when it stops for a while on the top and moves back and forth, you I want to come down. You have to learn to steady the motion instead of giving in.

Field—It's all right to play the field, but make sure you remember to cultivate once in a while.

Field Goal—They put too much pressure on a field goal kicker in a game. If the rest of the team would do their part, the game wouldn't depend on whether the kicker makes the field goal or not.

Fifth Wheel—Don't feel bad if people consider you a fifth wheel, because when one of the other wheels goes flat, look who they turn to.

Fighting—Peace is so much better.

Figure—Don't become so obsessed about how you look that it deters you from living a normal life. If you can move around and talk, be thankful.

Figure Skating—The best-shaped bodies in the world belong to figure skaters. They know what hard work is all about.

File Clerk—This job is crucial, because important paperwork must be filed in the right place for future reference.

Final—Nothing is final until the fat lady sings, and if you see her start to sing, tell her not to come back until she loses some weight.

Fine—If you are fine, quit complaining.

Fine-tooth Comb—Somethings you can go over with a fine-tooth comb, while for other things it takes a coarse pitchfork.

Finger—Don't point your finger at anybody. Your fingers are meant for doing, not pointing.

Fingernail—Fingernails have a rough life. They're bitten, cut, painted all sorts of colors, and grown sometimes to extreme lengths. But worst of all, they're used sometimes to scratch in the most unusual places.

Finish—Don't start anything you can't finish, because the finish line was meant to cross, not to avoid.

Finishing School—It may train you for life in society, but when life gets done with you, you will feel like your training was from dingdong school.

Fire extinguisher—Keep one handy and learn how to use it. The lives of you and your loved ones are too precious to allow to go up in smoke.

Fire Fighters—They risk their lives everyday, so show kindness and gratitude to them every day.

Firing Squad—You know a person's luck ran out if after being the first person shot, the firing squad had a change of heart and pardoned everybody left in line.

Firmness—Be firm in life, but don't rule out being gentle if your firmness proves to be too much for the situation at hand.

First—It doesn't matter where you place, just so you give it your best.

Firstborn—The oldest in a family has a lot of pressure. They have to set the example for the rest of their siblings to follow.

First Lady—It doesn't matter if you are the first lady or the last lady, as long as you remember to be a lady.

Fish—Fish are helpless out of water, and so are humans who neglect their lungs for one more puff.

Fisherman—You don't have to be a fisherman to tell a fish story. Some of the best stories come from non-fisherman.

Five-and-dime—Now your stores are more like it takes the whole body to buy something.

Flag—Be proud of it; the ones who fought for it were.

Flash Card—One of the most powerful tools of learning. It may be simple compared to a computer, but the mind has to react quickly. A quick mind developed at a young age becomes a smart one at an older age.

Flat—Know how to change a tire when you have a flat, because sometimes the stranger you ask for help might leave you flat like your tire.

Flesh—Take care of your flesh, because it is the makeup for your bones.

Flesh and Blood—No matter how important you think a person is, we are all just flesh and blood. Even the president of the United States.

Flight Attendant—The greatest asset they have is their smile. A smile can erase the fear and anxiety of flying. Their smile is the airiest welcome mat in the world.

Float—Watch a parade and see the hard work that went into the floats. It is known was a labor of love.

Flock—Be part of the flock, for without them you are not as strong as you could be.

Flood—The way some people act, I think Noah saved too many jackasses on the ark.

Floor—Don't wax your floors so much that your local little league team wants to hold sliding practice on your kitchen floor.

Florist—They provide the joy or comfort people need.

Flower—Send some to somebody who needs a bouquet of love to make it through the night.

Fly Off—Better to get a handle on something than to fly off the handle.

Focus—Focus your eyes on things that will enlighten your world, not darken it.

Fog—If the fog level in your head is too high, remember to turn your headlights on.

Folk Song—Songs you can understand the words to. You don't need a dictionary to understand the lyrics.

Follow—Follow your dreams, and if you come to a dead end, build your own overpass and keep going.

Food—Don't deny people the power to think for themselves. The lack of food does this to people. Help to see that everybody has the food needed to be an independent, thinking human being.

Foolproof—Something may be foolproof today, but tomorrow you can send in the clowns.

Foot—Take care of your feet; look at the weight they have to carry.

Football—People get excited about the Super Bowl. But I have never seen where because of this game being played, that a cure for cancer or some other disease had been found. Let's support the ones looking for a cure as much as we support the Super Bowl.

Force—Don't use force unless in self-defense or when somebody else is in trouble.

Foreman—A tough job, because you are in between those who like you and those who dislike you.

Forest Ranger—Smokey the Bear's greatest friend as far as protecting the forest goes. Appreciate them, because without people like them, the survival of nature would be in greater risk sooner than you think.

Forget—If you are having a hard time remembering things, see a doctor. The key to make it through the night is remembering the good times.

Forgive—If our father in heaven can forgive you when you sin, you too can forgive those who trespass against you.

Fortune—It doesn't take a fortune to enjoy the sun, stars, ocean, etc. The best things in life really are free.

Fortuneteller—Trust in God. Let him take care of the future.

Forty—They say life begins at forty. If I would have known for sure, I would have played hooky until then.

Forty-niner—With the greed for money today, if there was gold in those hills, the forty-niners wouldn't have a chance. They would be run over by the mob in their sport cars racing to see who gets there first.

Forty Winks—No matter how long or how little you sleep, if you sleep the wrong way you may wake up with forty kinks.

Forward—March on towards your goal and place in the sun.

Foul Ball—Don't knock a foul ball in baseball, because to some hitters it represents their greatest achievement.

Foundation—Build a strong foundation, and if you ever fall in the gutter, you will have the strength to pull yourself out.

Founding Fathers—I don't think they would like the dirty political campaigns of today. I bet they would love to come back and wash a few politicians' mouths out with soap.

Foundry—Bless those who work in a foundry. It is hard and hot work.

Fourth of July—Let's extend our hand across the world and let freedom ring for all mankind.

Frame—Be in the right frame of mind every day, and you can accomplish anything.

Freak—If you think somebody is a freak, maybe you should take a good look at yourself once in the mirror.

Free Agent—A lot of these become moneybags in U.S.A.

Freedom—America. What else can I say?

Freezing Point—When Hell loses its touch.

French Door—Behind this door some French lovers go *oui-oui*, and occasionally some French dogs go pee-pee.

Fresh—Be fresh in the morning and clear-headed, and you will be a member of the team with the best ideas.

Fresh water—You can forget about this if the environment goes to hell.

Friday—The day God is thanked for more than any other day of the week.

Friend—Be a friend to somebody who doesn't have one.

Frigid—Don't be frigid, there is time for that when you are six feet under.

Frisk—A good frisk is one that will take your mind off your troubles.

Front page—Your life may not be on the front page, but in God's eyes you are a frontpage edition.

Frown—Don't frown when a smile would do you and everybody else you meet so much good.

Fruit cake—If you receive a fruitcake for a gift and you aren't too crazy about it, there is a way to check to see if it's safe to eat. Roll it down a hill. If it's too light it will roll ahead of you; if it's too heavy, it will lag behind you; and if it's just right, it will keep up with you.

Frustration—This only causes a waste of time in getting something accomplished.

Fuel—If people would put as much effort into their work as they do when it comes to quitting time, think of what could be accomplished. The products of America would be so good, there wouldn't be any competition from foreign markets. "Made in the USA" would be just as common a phrase as "Born in the USA."

Full—Remember to keep your tank full, especially at night and in the wintertime.

Fumble—Don't worry if you are a football player and you fumble the football in a game. How in the hell can you hold on to it when you are hit by an elephant?

Funeral Home—Have you ever walked into a funeral home and thought there was a party going on? Why does it take a person's departing before some people arrive on the scene.

Fun House—This is a fun house where a family doesn't fight; they show respect and love towards one another. They have fun and a great time together.

Funnel—Funnel your love to where it is needed the most.

Funny Bone—How can they tell which bone is your funny bone? Does it laugh at a precise time?

Fur—Nice to see an animal run by instead of a dead one hung over somebody's body.

Furnish—Be the provider you were meant to be, and you will see results that will provide you with a smile.

Fury—Don't be like the fury of a storm when the calmness of the sea will accomplish so much more.

Future—Your future depends upon what you do today.

Gadabout—This type of person should go to a nursing home and provide some excitement for the residents there instead of seeking it for himself or herself.

Gagman—Some politicians don't need to hire a gagman. They are their own gagman.

Gain—Earn your place in the sun, and when the sun's rays shine on you, you know the warmth was meant for you.

Galaxy—The greatest place and the highest place to be. Let's hope man doesn't destroy it by nuclear war, because it is our greatest hope of all for peace.

Gallery—So what if your paintings aren't in a gallery? You paint because you enjoy it, not to impress others

Gambling—Excessive gambling means the loss of the chance to live right, so quit while you are ahead and live right again.

Game—A game is meant for fun and enjoyment, not for blood, sweat and tears.

Game Warden—They protect what could be lost to nature forever because of man's greed for more. So appreciate them for the beauty they preserve.

Gang—I wish all would gangs would work for the goodwill of their community instead of inflicting harm on one another.

Gangplank—If you can swim, going off the gangplank it isn't so bad.

Gap—If you don't spend enough communication time with your children now, you will experience a communication gap down the line. So listen and speak to your children and respect their status in life.

Garbage—What we consider garbage is a gourmet dinner to hungry people.

Garden—May the seeds of life you plant produce the accomplishments of tomorrow you desire.

Garlic—Eat this to keep undesirables away.

Garter Belt—This went out with the horse and buggy. I think.

Gate—Have a gate on your yard, but don't close the gate to your mind.

Gather—Let us all gather together and send a message of peace to the rest of the world.

Gear—Be sure your gears are oiled up. You never can tell when you have to go into action.

Geisha—Be sure you know what the girl under the makeup looks like before you take her out on a date.

Generate—Generate good will around you and hope it spreads.

Generation—Let's hope for generation after generation that peace will reign supreme all over the world.

Generous—Be generous to those who don't have as much.

Genius—Everybody is smart in his or her own way.

Gentle—Be gentle, and you will see more smiles greet you everyday.

Gentleman—Marry one, and you will see the difference between a gentleman and a not-so-a gentleman.

Geography—Learn the universe around you and get to know the people living in other countries. When you learn about God's other children, you get to know yourself better as a human being.

Germ—Stop germs in their tracks: wash your hands after a nature call.

Geyser—Use your brainpower to the highest gush you can.

Ghost—Don't give up the ghost until you see one.

Gifted—Everybody is gifted. We are all gifted by being ourselves to the best of our abilities, if we put forth the effort.

Gigantic—Be a giant helper to those too small to help themselves.

Gin Rummy—Better to play a card game than to drink too much gin. Drink too much gin, and you will be dancing the samba backwards.

Girdle—It's time for a new one when you start getting vibes from your girdle in places you never dreamed of.

Girl Scouts—They teach girls the good things in life and how to live right.

Give—Give until it hurts, then you will be satisfied you did your part in making the world a better place for all.

Give-and-take—It's all right to give and take, but make sure there is something left after all the giving and taking for you to enjoy.

Glad—Be glad if you can get out of bed in the morning and be the person God wants you to be.

Gladiator—They fought with sword and lived with the sword and some died because of the sword. The moral of the story is: don't get all sworded out.

Glad Rags—Give some glad rags that you don't need anymore to the needy, and for them they will become their survival rags.

Glass Blowing—A beautiful trade because it beautifies the world.

Glee Club—Join a glee club if you want to sing. The joy you bring others is worth all the practice time. I wanted to sing in the glee club in high school, but some older kids kept picking on me, so I quit. I wasn't very brave when I was young. What I should have done was turn around and punch them in the nose. When you want to do something, never give in to the stupidity of others.

Glitter—All that glitters isn't gold, but enjoy the sparkle anyway.

Globe—Buy one for your house if you don't have one and discover the world.

Glory—Glory of God is always.

Glove—Some people whom you have to handle with kid gloves should have a good kick in the behind instead.

Goaltender—No matter how many goals are scored against him or her, it is a hard job. It's like having your mother-in-law firing at you with a machine gun.

Godparent—A good one will see to it that their godchild lives the kind of life that will make the parents proud.

Going—Go where your heart desires.

Gold—Being happy is not having as much gold as Fort Knox. Being happy is the years you make golden by the fond memories of your past, your present, and your future.

Goldfish—They bring happiness to people because life in a fishbowl was meant for fish, not people.

Gold Rush—If more people would work at their job like the people who were in the gold rush, "Made in the USA" would mean something.

Golf—If they would make the holes as big as bushel baskets, I'm sure more people would play it.

Good—Be good and see the joy your goodness brings to others.

Good-bye—Never think of this as farewell, because you have to meet someone before you can say good-bye. Remember the meeting, not the parting.

Good Looks—Everyone is good-looking in his or her own way.

Goose—Don't goose anybody, or the goose you cook may be your own.

Gospel—Live the gospel, and your life will preach to the whole world.

Gossip—Don't feel bad if people gossip about you. If they are talking about you, then they aren't talking about someone else. So you are great.

Governess—Leave your child too long in the care of another person, and he or she will start calling her mother.

Gown—It isn't the person who is dressed the nicest at the prom that counts, it's the person who can be himself or herself without putting up a front.

Graduate—If you didn't have an opportunity to go to college, high school, or even grade school, don't feel bad. Everyday you live you advance as a human being.

Grain—Help the family farms so that the grain can be grown that feeds us.

Grammar—Don't worry about the level of grammar you use, just be thankful you can talk.

Grandparents—Grandparents like to brag about their grandchildren, but don't feel bad if you don't have any. It isn't the number of grandchildren you have that counts; it's the love you show towards children who don't have anybody else to love them.

Grand-slam—Life is like a grand-slam; the home run is just the beginning. You have to make it around all the bases and tag them. What a feeling, though, when you tag home plate. Dying is nothing to be afraid of. You are just tagging home plate and looking forward to the applause you deserve.

Grass—Don't worry about how green your lawn is when there is a drought going on. Think about the farmers and the crops they raise for us to eat.

Grasshopper—Some people are so jumpy they could give grasshoppers a run for their money in head to head competition.

Gravestone—You don't need a fancy saying on your tombstone. People who lead a good life according to the will of God, will be remembered by others as good examples for the rest of the world to follow.

Greasepaint—Some women wear too much makeup and it looks like greasepaint. P.S. Some men do, too, especially during a political debate.

Greatest—I once thought the greatest thing you could be in life was the president, movie star, or a king or queen, but that isn't true. The greatest thing you can be in your life is yourself to the best of your ability. That is all the master desires you to be.

Greedy—Be greedy, but for the needy.

Greenhorn—Give a greenhorn a break. They have to start somewhere.

Green Thumb—Some people have killer thumbs: a knack for having plants die on them all the time.

Greyhound—I like the Greyhound bus, and I think the greyhound dog makes a good pet. But I don't think they should be used for racing. Let them use their legs for their own enjoyment, not for the purpose of increasing the green of precious few.

Grief—Overcome your grief with prayers from your heart.

Grill—Slave over a hot one in a busy restaurant, and you will know what hard work is all about.

Grizzly Bear—Be careful if you wake up feeling like a grizzly bear and you choose to go to work with that feeling. You co-workers might call the local zoo and ask for tranquilizer gun and a cage.

Grocer—Be thankful they have to buy. Without them, the world would be too slim for comfort.

Groom—Don't get too nervous and wait too long to go down the aisle, otherwise it might just be you and the minister going off in the sunset.

Ground—With your feet flat on the ground and a firm grip on yourself, grind out your problems, and your troubles will go away.

Group—A unit of people, with each one capable of thinking as an individual.

Grow—Everyday we grow as people. Why not as humanity.

Grudge—Don't hold a grudge so long that your purpose for living is lose.

Guard—Use your defense against sin and keep the scoreboard saying zero on the bad side.

Guernsey—I think Guernsey cows are beautiful. They remind one of the foundation of America: the family farm.

Guide—Be the guide dog to those who have lost sight of their goals in life.

Guided Missile—One of these shot off by a fool is one fool-guided missile too many.

Guinea Pig—If you are being used as a guinea pig, find out what you are being experimented on for before you become a dead duck.

Gullible—A person who rolls around the ground, wrapped only in a sheet soaked in milk, after hearing a news report it helps prevent heart attacks if done after midnight.

H

Habit—Develop good habits, and you will find yourself living a better life.

Hacienda—It's okay to rest at your hacienda as long as you don't make your senora or senorita do all the work.

Hail—Hail, hail, the gang's all here, and when they come, greet them with open arms. Have a party and serve non-alcoholic drinks, but be sure to keep the noise down so that you don't disturb the neighbors.

Hair—Don't worry if you are losing your hair. Your brainpower doesn't go down because of it. Also, if you think your sex appeal is going out of the window because of your hair loss, you have to lot to learn. How you perform is your sex appeal.

Hairpiece—Make sure after a windstorm your hairpiece isn't one of the casualties.

Halfback—Those who play football are courageous people, because you have to be able to endure pain and you never know who is going to hit you next.

Half-baked—Some people are half-baked. Those are the people who are mean to other people and animals and don't give a hoot how they litter and destroy the property of others.

Hallmark—They bring happiness to others through their cards.

Hall of Fame—Don't feel bad if you don't make it into the Hall of Fame, because we all belong to the most important hall of all: the Hall of Life.

Halo—Some people would like to put halos on their heads, but they don't fit because of their horns.

Halt—Put a stop to things that corrupt the minds of children.

Hand—Shake hands with a friend and say, "Peace be with you," and tell them to pass it on.

Handicap—A person may be bodily handicapped, but nothing can handicap his or her spirit.

Handkerchief—Don't be afraid to use a Kleenex or a handkerchief to blow your nose, no matter what sex you are. Don't let society dictate to you what stands for femininity and what stands for masculinity.

Handle—Don't fly off the handle when being in control of the handle will produce better results.

Handmade—Appreciate anything handmade, because a lot of love and labor went into making it.

Hand-me-down—Hand-me-downs may be your most prized processions, because they have been tried, tested, and have lasted.

Handout—Don't be afraid to take a handout. From it you can gain strength to be in the position to help somebody else who is in need of help, too.

Handshake—Don't judge a person by his or her handshake. Some people have the strength to shake more firmly than others.

Handsome—It's all right to be good-looking, but don't let your good looks change how you treat other people. Beauty built from within doesn't change with age like beauty on the outside does.

Handwriting—Your handwriting may be bad, but at least you can express your mind.

Hangover—When your head feels like the Empire's State Building.

Happy—You have only two choices in life: to be happy or not to be happy. You are in control of what you choose. Why would anyone choose to be unhappy?

Happy-go-lucky—The sunshine within this type of person outshines the real sun in nature. Even on rainy days, the sun within happy-go-lucky people is shining.

Hardball—Many political campaigns are based on this. What example is this for the youth of the world?

Hard Hat—The people who wear these are brave, because they build the heights that we look up to.

Harmony—If everybody worked together, war would be obsolete.

Has-been—Nobody is a has been. They are just in a different phase of their life.

Haste—Don't make haste if it means leaving a mess a mile long.

Hat—Make sure when you pass the hat that you get it back.

Haunt—Don't allow your memories to haunt you. What is done is done.

Hay fever—People who suffer from this have many a happy day ruined by burning eyes and running noses. So be patient and understanding as they reach for their Kleenex or handkerchief.

Head—Use it to your fullest potential, and people won't accuse you of having an attic for rent.

Headache—Don't fake one because to people who get them all the time, headaches are not so funny.

Headfirst—Some people who dive headfirst into a swimming pool have the ability to bounce right back to the diving board.

Headline—Your daily life may not make the headlines, but you are a headliner in God's world.

Hearing Aid—Don't be afraid to wear a hearing aid if you need one. A lot of precious moments of life are lost because they aren't heard.

Heart—Sometimes it takes trying from the bottom of your heart to show the love of which you are capable.

Heart Attack—Be sure to exercise and eat the right kind of food, and then maybe you can avoid this. Also learn CPR if you don't know how to do it. The more you learn about your heart, the more you yourself and others if the occasion ever arises.

Heartthrob—One person's heartthrob may be another person's heartache.

Heaven—A place where dreams come true.

Heavyweight—Be a heavyweight for the needy and homeless and deliver the knockout punch to eliminate their troubles forever.

Heel—Some people are heels, so don't let them become your shoes.

Height—It doesn't matter how tall you are. Your ideas will make up for lack of height.

Heimlich Maneuver—Learn this life-saving maneuver, and if the need ever arises to use it, you can save a life and help a person live to his or her fullest potential.

Heir—To inherit another person's good qualities is a far greater value than money. One you can take with you, the other one you can't.

Hell—The saying "until hell freezes over" is not true. It should be "until hell smothers out."

Hello—Saying hello to a depressed person does more good to him or her than a trip to a psychiatrist.

Helmsman—You are the helmsman of your ship. Steer it with the best effort you can.

Hemline—Wear your hemline as short or as long as you want. Don't let the mainstream of society dictate you how to wear your clothes.

Hercules—If you can't look like Hercules, then think like Einstein. The strength of the mind can move mountains.

Heredity—Never blame your mistakes on heredity. You are an individual, so be responsible for yourself.

Hermit—You are never alone, because God is everywhere.

Hero—Everybody is a hero. Getting up every morning and facing the world takes courage beyond compare.

Heroin—Life is confusing enough, don't add to the confusion by taking drugs.

Hesitate—Don't take too long to decide something because opportunity might pass you by.

Hide-and-seek—We used to play this as kids. Now some adults play it when they commit a crime and hide from the police and the police seek them out. Don't let the crimes in life ruin the games in life.

High—Get high on the playing field, not while driving a car.

High Rise—A lot of senior citizens live in a high rise, so don't look down on them for getting old, because they can now look down on you from their living-room windows.

Highway—I think there should be separate highways for those who insist on driving while drunk or speeding down the highway. The rest of us could drive on the other highway and have peace of mind at the same time.

Hike—If somebody tells you to go and take a hike, ask him or her how far you should go.

Hillbilly—A lot of hillbillies have more common sense than the so-called sophisticated people.

Hinder—Never hinder anyone or anything unless hindrance is the key in preventing a mistake for somebody or something.

Hippopotamus—Life would be fun if you could eat as much as you like without worrying about getting fat. Look at hippopotamuses; they eat as much as they like and they have fun and wallow in the mud.

The moral of the story. Don't judge people or things by their size. Life can be fun no matter what size you are.

Hispanic—They have a proud heritage. Respect it.

History—In the history books, all the presidents of the United States are listed, but everybody —past, present and future—is a part of history, so know that you have made a contribution to society.

Hit—Hit only in self-defense.

Hit-and-run—Life is precious; don't disregard it by doing this.

Hitchhiker—Don't hitchhike or pick up a hitchhiker, otherwise you may be using your fingers for something else: to protect yourself.

Hobby—If you are bored with your life, take up a hobby, and you will turn boring time into joy time.

Hobbyhorse—If you see an adult rocking on a hobbyhorse, it could be a politician running for office, depressed used car salesman, or it could be an adult who wanted one as a child and this is a dream come true.

Hogwash—Some of the greatest ideas were considered this before they became million-dollar success stories.

Hole—Sometimes when you are in a hole, you have to dig deeper before you can get out.

Hollywood—Where people get paid for doing things in movies that in real life they would get arrested for.

Hollywood Bed—One that sleeps dirty and sexy.

Holocaust—The memory and spirit of those lost in the Holocaust will live forever.

Home—Have you ever gotten mad about something or mad at somebody and said, "They can wait until the cows come home"? That can be a long time, because the cows stop sometimes on the way home and have a bull session.

Homecoming—The time to welcome home those who have been away too long.

Homeless—Why not give aid to the homeless? We treat them as foreigners, so we could call it foreign aid. The way our government gives out foreign aid, they would have money galore.

Homemaker—An important career and don't let anybody tell you otherwise.

Homestretch—Where your undertaking becomes the final push for tomorrow.

Homework—Too much homework kills the fun of life, so teachers lighten up a little bit and let some fun shine back into your students' lives.

Homosexual—Live and let live. Let God judge what is right and what is wrong. He earned that right by dying on the cross.

Honesty—The freedom of the truth will always set you free, so let freedom ring.

Honeymoon—The honeymoon is over when your lovemaking sessions are counted by the years instead of the days.

Hooray—Hooray for Hollywood when they make a clean, family picture.

Hope—Live today because of the hope of tomorrow.

Hope Chest—The rich person's version of this is an entire floor at a department store.

Horse—A horse may wear blinders, but don't let the blinders in life keep you from seeing anything.

Horseradish—The greatest sinus-opener in the world.

Hospital—When it comes to nighttime for the patients, some are like a library, while some others are like a party waiting to happen.

Hostage—How come when terrorists hijack a plane, most of the time they let everybody go except the men? Some of the women could handle the terrorists just as well as the men. Men aren't emotionally strong all the time, and women aren't emotionally weak all the time.

Hot dog—A hot dog you should try is a Coney Island. I think it was named after Coney Island in New York. It is delicious.

Hotheaded—This type of person should eat more hotdogs. This would make him or her joyous and give them energy to be more hotfooted in the pursuit of cooler goals.

Hourglass—What a tranquil way to watch time trickle by.

Home—A house is not a home until you have a foundation of love.

House Arrest—This is a house arrested for having its shades up while sexual activity of the occupants is going on.

Houseboat—The symbol of relaxing the way it was meant to be enjoyed.

Housefly—Some of these seem big when they are pestering a person; they give elephants competition as far as size goes.

Household Name—Everybody is this in God's world.

Housewife—I sometimes think this is an incorrect statement, because a woman is not married to her house.

Housework—This is not identified by gender, so everybody living under the same roof should pitch in and do his or her share, big and small.

How—Don't ask how; just do it. Doing is learning in action.

Hubcap—The way they make hubcaps nowadays, they are getting to be more valuable than your local jewelry store.

Hug—Hug someone special when they need reassurance of your love for them.

Hula Hoop—I think they should bring the hula hoop back. Nobody would have to worry about being overweight if they exercised with it.

Human Brain—The computer is trying to replace this, but it will never make the grade, because something God-made excels something man-made every time.

Humble—Eat some humble pie, but leave some for someone else, because you're not alone.

Humor—Add some cheer to your life and make others laugh.

Humorless—Some women become this when at work they realize they forgot to put their makeup on. For some men it's when they realize at work they forgot to put their toupee when their head starts feeling cold.

Hunchback—Walk proudly if you have a humped back. You have nothing to ashamed of.

Hurdle—Learn to jump, and you will be able to jump any hurdle that comes your way in life.

Hurricane—People who survive one of these know what a storm is all about.

Hurt—Don't do anything to anybody that you wouldn't want done to yourself.

Hush Puppies—The shoes that make walking a pleasant experience.

Hygiene—Do your share to promote health and prevent disease. Practise good health care.

Hyperactive—Have patience and hope for the best if you have a hyperactive child. Trust in the Lord and find a good doctor for your child.

Hypnosis—Don't be so open to suggestions that you cant think for yourself.

Hysterical—Being calm in certain situations would serve you better than excessive fear or panic.

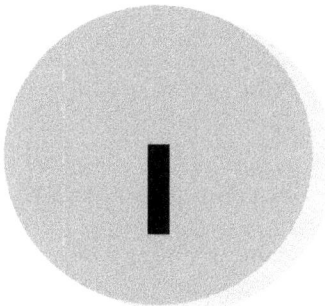

Ice Age—I think some of the people from the ice age must have thawed out wrong, when you take a good look at some of their kin running around today.

Ice Hockey—Only one fight during a game is one too many for the bad example it gives the youth of the world.

Ice-Skate—Ice-Skate for the fun of it, and then will come the green to prove the reality of it.

Icing—Not everybody react to the same situations that are alike. To some it is icing on the cake, while some others may think it's duck soup, but to some it's like taking their mother-in-law on their honeymoon.

Ideas—Don't let your ideas go to waste. Act on them, and you will see the fruits of your labor.

Identity Crisis—Normal growing process. If it gets too serious, seek professional help. Know your own identity, and people will recognize you for yourself and not somebody else's style. When you know yourself you have a friend for life.

Idle—Idle time is the devil's workshop. I sometimes think the way the world is, his workshop must be over-flowing.

Igloo—Don't become so cold that you remind people of an igloo.

Ignition—May the ignition of your career goals be fired up and ready to go at all times.

Illegal—It should be made illegal for a band to have to march behind horses in a parade. How can they win a trophy if they are slipping all over the place?

Illiterate—If you have the time, help those who can't read or write. A reading nation is a leading nation.

Illness—If you are sick and aren't getting better, see your doctor and put your faith in the doctor of all God.

Illustrate—Set an example for others to follow as you journey through life.

Imitation—Don't be an imitation of yourself. People want to see the real you, so be yourself to your fullest potential.

Immediate—If the world would try to be one big immediate family, we would not have to worry about war.

Immigrants—Make them feel like they are at home.

Immunization—Protect yourself against anything that would want to see you succumb to the temptations of evil. A warehouse of grace built up in your soul is the greatest immune system of all.

Impatience—Learn to wait your turn in life, and you will be ready to do your best in life.

Impeach—Everybody can be replaced, no matter what office they hold. Only God can't be replaced.

Impede—Obstruct Satan as he tries to spread his evil work on earth.

Important—I don't care how important a person is or thinks he or she is. When they die, the world will keep on going. Look at the president of the United States; the world doesn't stop for him or her when they die.

Impose—Don't place a burden on anybody if you can help it. Take care of your own obligations, and if you have some strength left over, help someone else.

Impossible—Anything is possible if you set your mind to it.

Imposter—Somebody who appears nice but behind closed doors is a spouse beater, or a child abuser, or cruel to animals, etc.

Impractical—Trying to make an elephant and a donkey march together in a parade. There would be too BS between them; they would slow down the parade.

Impression—Make a good imprint on somebody's mind, and you will be a source of delight for them whenever they see you.

Imprison—Not all prisons have bars on them. Sometimes we suffer from the imprisonment of our minds.

Impromptu—It's never a bad time to discuss the needs of others.

Improper—Always show good taste, and your way of doing things will be accepted by those that could make a difference in your life.

Improve—Make better what you can; accept what you can't.

Impulse—Make sure the force you exert pushes you in the right direction.

Inauguration—When the outfit the woman holding the Bible wears receives more attention than the man being sworn in. Time will come when the roles will be reversed. The woman will be the one being sworn in. The first gentleman holding the Bible will make the only fashion statement he can; a suit with an overcoat if it's cold.

Incest—Help is needed for both the victim and the perpetrator. Report it if you see it or if it is happening to you. Silence is not golden when it comes to incest.

Include—Include those people in your life who have no friends.

Income Tax—The payroll check paper shredder.

Incomplete—Your life will be incomplete until you fulfill it to the fullest.

Increase—Increase your will power to become a better person, and the world will become a better place.

In Crowd—Don't feel bad if you don't belong to the in crowd. Some of the people who belong to the in crowd would have to go to a dark room with a flashlight to find their brains.

Incubator—The miracle machine that does its thing to save the miracle child.

Incumbent—Different from the very first time the politician runs for office. They go a step up the ladder on campaign money. Instead of peanuts, they have cashews.

Incurable—Anything can be cured as long as the mind hangs on to hope.

Independence Day—When freedom became a reality in American for generations to enjoy forever.

Independent—Be this way, but be willing to accept help when you need it.

Indian summer—The summer that means more than the regular summer.

Indoors—Indoors can be just as much fun as the outdoors. You just have to adapt to things according to the environment around you.

Indulge—Eat all the sweets you want, but it is time to stop when you have more rolls than your local bakery.

Inequality—Everybody is born equal, whether everyone believes it or not. Along the way, some people's thinking got mixed up and they don't accept this, but it doesn't change the fact.

Infant—The impression you leave on a child's mind at this stage is the indelible mark they will leave on society when they grow up.

Inferiority Complex—Get help if this makes you feel like a fish out of water.

Infidelity—If you can forgive, you can forget.

Infielder—A good one stays limber and keeps his or her eyes on the ball at all times.

Inform—Keep your self informed of the events going on around you all the time. The more informed you are, the more likely you are of obtaining your American dream.

Inherit—What you earn on your own is more valuable than what you wait for.

Inhumane—If everybody would do his or her part to spread kindness, we could eliminate this.

Injustice—Try to correct the unfairness in the world. Where there is injury, be the healing bandage needed for the wound.

Inkwell—Don't let your well dry. Keep a ready reserve on hand. If you think you can dry pen it, you are kidding yourself.

Innocent—Protect the innocent, for they are the children of tomorrow.

Insane—I think everybody has to act a little bit cuckoo once in a while in order to survive in life nowadays.

Insect—Sometimes the smallest creatures in the world have the greatest power.

Insignificant—People who bother you.

Inspiration—People who don't bother you.

Instinct—Use your instinct to seek the right values as you wage war against the struggles in your life.

Institution—Visit one and, when you come out, count your blessings.

Instruction—Instruct those people who need help in obtaining their goals in life.

Instrument—Be an instrument of peace so that you do your part for all of Gods' children to live in peace.

Insurance—This costs too much, and when you try to collect it, you can't bank on anything.

Intelligence—We are all born with it. Everybody is smart in his or her own way. We just have to learn how to develop it. Different levels of intelligence do not mean one person is smart and the next person is dumb.

Intent—Don't be afraid to change your mind if your intentions don't serve the purpose you had in mind.

Interest—Let your interests be your guide in obtaining what is best for you.

Interference—Interference is necessary when you think it will do some good for somebody.

Interior—Let the interior of your heart be coated with the kind of love that can be dispensed with a moment's notice.

Interview—Don't be nervous at an interview. Be yourself and let your inner self shine through.

Introduction—Don't be afraid to say who you are, because nobody can be you better than you can.

Intent—Keep your mind creative as much as possible.

Investment—Make strong investments, because they are what you live on when the time comes.

Involve—Involve yourself with projects that will make the whole world better.

Irish Whiskey—Drink too much of this, and you will be able to sing, "Oh Danny Boy" backwards without missing a beat.

Ironing Board—Don't let it bother you if are flatchested. Some women who have had their breasts removed because of cancer are living normal and productive lives.

Island—No man or woman is an island, but sometimes it takes thinking like an island to survive the mainland.

Issue—Take up the issue where justice hasn't been met, because you live in America and you have that right.

Itinerary—May your plan for life include thanking God for the blessings bestowed on you.

Ivory Tower—A bunch of elephants standing on top of one another.

Jack—Jack up your life everyday by putting forth the best effort you can.

Jack Frost—Be prepared, so when Jack Frost blows cold air in your ace, you are able to respond by blowing hot air back at him. You do his by wearing warm clothes and having your car prepared for winter.

Jam Session—A good time to blend and combine the talents of musicians for the enjoyment of all.

Janitors—They make the floor we take for granted sparkle—those floors we never notice until they are dirty. Why not thank all the janitors when the floors are clean, instead of birching when they are dirty?

Jawbreaker—A steak well-done to the point of extreme.

Jealousy—Jealousy doesn't serve any purpose except to demean you as a human being.

Jekyll and Hyde—Some politicians after they get into office.

Jerks—Jerks are developed, not born, so don't let this development overtake you.

Jesus—He died so that we could live.

Jet lag—When you sleepwalk off the plane, your body can't tell whether it's constipated or has diarrhea, and your watch has had a nervous break down.

Jet Set—If you feel comfortable riding in the caboose, why worry about the jets flying overhead? It doesn't matter what your style is; just enjoy it. You are the one living with it.

Jewel—Be the jewel that God meant you to be.

Jigsaw Puzzle—Don't feel bad if your life is like a jigsaw puzzle. When puzzle is solved, look how nicely everything fits together, and the picture of your life is delightful to the eye.

Job—What some have and wish they didn't, and what some don't have and wish they did.

Journalism—Tell the truth when you write something, and the right you write will be all right.

Journey—Make your journey through life a pleasant one. Take one day at a time and you will make it through the night.

Joy Ride—Don't take too many of these, otherwise your next ride may be in a hearse instead.

Jubilee—Plan a special anniversary celebration for the dear one in your life.

Judas—Make sure your own front porch is swept clean before you accuse anybody else of being a betrayer.

Judges—I wish judges wouldn't throw cases out on technicalities, because I think of all the hard police work that went into them.

Judgment Day—On this day God is going to give out Oscars even Hollywood can't match. They will be for the people who helped others when they probably needed help themselves.

Jukebox—It preserves the music that you can understand the words to and lets you swing to your style of music.

Jumbo Jet—It is nice to take a jet, but in biblical times they traveled by donkey. Don't knock it. I never heard of a donkey crashing.

Jump—The saying that everybody puts his pants on one leg at a time is not true. Some people get a running start and jump into their pants.

Jumper Cable—If the love from your heart has stopped, use a jumper cable and let it flow again.

Jungle—It can be a jungle out there, but if you take it one day at a time, you can thin it out a little.

Junior College—A good place to learn what career will suit you the best.

Junk—Remember, you are good; God doesn't make any junk.

Junkyard—Some of life's greatest values can be found here. They are known as memories.

Jupiter—Where all the political conventions should be held.

Kangaroo—I think kangaroos are wonderful to watch as they jump around all over. If you could ger that much movement out of some people, you'd be lucky.

Karate—A battered woman should learn this. If a man starts to beat her, she could kick him where it would alter his sex life for a while.

Keep—Keep trying to do your best, and you will make out okay.

Key—The key to your success is if your heart, mind, and soul are up to the task and not just along for the ride.

Keynote Address—A good one will arouse you. A bad one will give Rip Van Winkle competition for the sleeping award.

Kindergarten—Where a first-rate teacher can develop first-rate minds.

Kindhearted—Kindhearted people leave a trail of goodies to benefit everybody.

King—There is only one, and He is the father of us all.

Kingdom—God's kingdom is there for you by answering the call to live right.

Kingpin—Anybody who thinks he is a kingpin should be careful of a bowling ball.

Kiss—Some people kiss and tell, others kiss and hide, some even kiss and die and those who don't kiss wonder what they miss.

Kiss of Death—Writing a bad check to the IRS.

Kitchen—There is a saying, "If you can't take the heat in the kitchen, get out." You don't have to do that, just open up a window.

Kite—If someone tells you to fly a kite, do it. You might enjoy it.

Kleenex—It's not a sign of weakness for a man to use a Kleenex. Being gentle to your nose makes more sense than using sandpaper.

Knickerbockers—Wear them if you enjoy them and bring back the carefree days and to hell with those who snicker at you. It is your life: wear what makes you happy.

Knockout—Don't let a knockout stop you in life. If the count of ten stops you in one event, just get on your feet and go on to the next event.

Knot—Tie a good one around hatred, and never let it go.

Know—Know that you are loved, even though people don't show it.

Knowledge—Build up your knowledge, and someday you will use it when you least expect it.

Knuckle—Don't be in the habit of giving out knuckle sandwiches unless you like the sight of field goal mouths.

Ku Klux Klan—To discriminate against one segment of society is to discriminate against all society. The brotherhood of man is society. You can't separate a whole as complete as that.

Labor—Make everything you do a labor of love, and the results will be music to your ears.

Labor Day—An important holiday because it honors the millions of workers who make America great. They may not make the headlines, but they are the force behind freedom for all.

Lack—If you lack something, work at it until it is at the level you want it to be.

Lady—A woman who knows inside she is polite, refined, and well-mannered, can take care of herself and isn't anybody's doormat, but doesn't have to put on a big front to prove it.

Lady-in-waiting—I don't know what this means. What are they waiting for? If they would say what, maybe somebody would help them.

Lamb—Some people are so fast it is like two shakes of a lamb's tail when they do something. For other people it's more like a bull's tail. No matter how fast or slow you do something, just be thankful that you can do it.

Lame Duck—Some politicians are this even before they start their political career.

Lampposts—Used to be the hookers who stood under lampposts, now you find the homeless.

Land—Wars are fought over land, which is lifeless and can't love. This is crazy, pure crazy. In wars people are killed, who were once alive and loved and are loved even today.

Landlocked—Don't let being enclosed by land stop you from dreaming about the sea, because dreams do come true. Before you know it, you will be sailing off into the sunset ready for the next sunrise in your life.

Landlord—Be a good one, and your tenants will respect you and lavish praise on you. You will gain a reputation for looking out for the little guy.

Landslide—If you win office by a landslide, make sure the good you do for your constituents is just as massive.

Lantern—May the lantern you light provide the light for some wayward soul.

Lap—Show love for your children by holding them in your lap once in a while. Of course, when they get too old and heavy for this, saying, "I love you" wouldn't hurt once in a while. If this is too hard for you to say, let your actions show you care.

Lapdog—Don't judge a dog by its size. Sometimes small dogs are the best protection in the world because of their noisy barks.

Laser—What a dream invention. The work that can be performed by a laser in the medical field is a miracle to behold.

Last—There's nothing wrong with last that first won't cure, because the Bible it says the last will be the first.

Last-ditch—Sometimes this is the best effort of all, because frantic thinking shakes up the brain.

Last Judgment—This is God's day, so don't try to start it on Earth.

Last Supper—The night before Christ died on the cross, when he poured forth His love for His fellow men one more time.

Late—Better late than never.

Laugh—Laugh when the occasion calls for it, because it is needed now more than ever.

Laundromat—Anybody who uses a Laundromat has the responsibility to use the machines properly and not cause damage to it. The owner of a Laundromat has the responsibility to see to it that the welfare of the customer is met, including watching out for people who have other things in mind besides washing and drying.

Lavatory—If you think life is hard now, just think, years ago there were no inside toilets and some people still live this way today.

Lawbreaker—Don't break the law unless you like counting bars to get to sleep.

Lawyer—A good one is worth his or her weight in gold, so take your time to find your gold mine. If you get a bad one, you never know how much of your bill is for hot air and how much is for quality.

Laxative—For some people who want to remain extremely thin, this a way of life. It is the only candy they know. This is sad, because the weight they want to be may be more deadly to them than the extra pounds they are afraid of.

Layoff—To be laid off from a job can demoralize you as a human being, but only let it be temporary. Get out there and present your resume and let the layoff be a memory to forget.

Lazy—Nobody is lazy; some people just have no desire to work.

Leach—The human ones are the hardest ones to get rid of.

Lead—They say you can lead a horse to water, but you can't make him or her drink it. That's not the only problem you have. Maybe you can't lead him or her back to where he or she came from. Then what do you do? You sure as hell can't give him or her a piggyback ride home.

Leaders—If it weren't for the followers, there wouldn't be anybody to lead. So appreciate those people behind you.

Leapfrog—A good game for lovers to find how agile one another are.

Learn—Everyday you learn something new, and your growth as a human being keeps on going.

Leatherneck—They are good at what they do, because discipline is an everyday occurrence for them.

Leave—Don't leave anybody or anything behind that you know can't take care of themselves.

Leaves—They are beautiful in the fall, but why don't we pay attention to them until they change colors? Why do we need change before we notice something? Why can't we accept things for what they are?

Left Field—Don't be afraid to express your opinion on something, even though some people may think it is way out in the left field. Maybe your opinion will become the mainstream of tomorrow.

Leg—The secret to life is to keep the legs moving.

Legends—In God's eyes, we are all legends.

Legislation—Follow your legislature and make sure your legislator votes for legislation that will be for the betterment of all mankind.

Legroom—For basketball players you need leg housing.

Legwork—Sometimes legwork is a better computer, because people's contact is better than machine contact.

Lemon—If the American car manufacturers would make better cars, the American people would not be forced to buy foreign ones.

Lenient—Be lenient when a too strict you may become an unmerciful you.

Lens—Take care of your eyes, because they are the camera that can give you the clearest picture.

Lent—Christ fasted for forty days and nights. Maybe we should try to match his sacrifice at least halfway.

Leopard—Protect them. Their spots are more beautiful on them than the two-legged creatures that wear coats made out of them.

Leotards—Good dancers make them come alive.

Leper—Courageous and brave is their heart and soul.

Leprechaun—If you see one of these, you better check what you had in your mulligan stew.

Lesson—Life is like a school. Learn your lessons. Do your homework and watch for your grades. If your grades are bad, you just have to work harder.

Letdown—Don't let up, and you won't suffer from a letdown in life.

Letter—Write a letter to someone who is lonely, and your words will fill his or her heart with the joy that he or she has been longing for.

Levelheaded—No matter what kind of head you have, just be thankful you have the power to think with it.

Liberal—They invented the instant cash machine, and when it runs out of money. They have the treasury department to print up some more money and let citizens of the USA pick up the tab.

Library—Read, and you will make the world a whole lot brighter and better place to live in.

Lie Detector—How can you tell whether a person is telling the truth or not when he or she has ice water in their veins.

Life—Don't take life too seriously: you're not going to get out of it alive.

Lifeguard—They serve to save, so give them a well-earned break and don't swim beyond your ability.

Life Preserver—Remember to wear one when you are in a boat. You are never too old for safety.

Lifestyle—Live the lifestyle that represents you and nor some imitation that reflects badly on you.

Lightning—They say lightning never strikes twice, but when you look at the way some people have their hair combed, something must have struck them.

Like—If you don't like somebody, it's not his or her problem, it's yours.

Lily of the Valley—I hope your valleys are filled with lilies to be used as stepping stones as you work your way up to the top again.

Limburger—Eat this when you want to be alone.

Limelight—We are all in the limelight of our lives.

Limit—There is a limit to everything, but don't let it stop you from making the progress you are working for in your life.

Limousine—Riding in a limousine doesn't make you important; it's what you do with your life when you step out of it that counts.

Line—Hold the line and walk the line, but don't skip the line.

Linebacker—They don't get any of the glory, but they are capable of dethroning the glory makers and putting them in their place.

Lineman—Be thankful that they are willing to work with power lines to keep our lives comfortable.

Lingerie—Wearing something sexy doesn't make you sexy; it has to come from within.

Linguist—Being able to speak several languages doesn't make you brilliant, it is working with the abilities you do have, whether it is being able to speak one language or ten languages.

Link—Make sure all your links are strong. Your hookup to life depends on it.

Lip Reading—Thanks for the courage of those people who learn lip reading. They let an impairment limit their life.

Lipstick—Be careful of lipstick on your collar, it could lead to the doghouse. That is, if Fido lets you in.

List—Don't feel bad if you don't have a list of friends a mile long. You can have the greatest friend of all, if you reach out to him. His name is Jesus Christ.

Literature—Read the right literature, write the right literature, and speak the right literature, and you will be prepared for life in a grand style.

Little—Don't judge people by their size. A lot of little people are shaping the world today.

Lively—Be lively. It is better than being deadly.

Living Room—A united family will have a relaxed feeling in this room. A broken family will have a restless feeling in this room. So for communication's sake, patch up your differences and relax as a family.

Load—Fill your head with knowledge and save it for a rainy day.

Loan—Don't borrow too much. The paying back can be killing if you don't have the money.

Lobbyist—Be remembered for your kindness, not your arm-twisting.

Local—The action starts at the local level before it spreads to the national level, so don't downplay the local touch.

Locker Room—Every reporter should be allowed to cover the sports story in the locker room, no matter the gender, the best talents should be able to write the best story. So players, don't turn your backs on what could be a field day in the sports pages for you.

Logic—Use it and enjoy it.

Logrolling—Too bad the differences in life couldn't be settled by a logrolling contest. The last one to stay on the log wins. Shootings and stabbings would go down. What shame the fists were replaced by guns and knives. The fists were bad enough.

Lonesome—Share your company with others, and your loneliness will be lost in the joy of doing volunteer work.

Long-distance—Beautiful memories can shorten the distance between you and your loved ones.

Long-winded—Some people are so long-winded you could nickname them sleeping pills, because they work better than a sleeping pill for putting people to sleep.

Look—Watch out for the booby traps in life.

Loons—The sound they make is worth more than some of the millions of words spoken everyday.

Loophole—When it comes to taxes, some people have so many loopholes, you could fly a whole fleet of 747s through them.

Lord's Day—It can be everyday for you if you do what the good book says.

Lord's Prayer—Say it to still your troubled mind.

Lose—You never lose something that you don't gain something from it.

Lost—Due to nuclear weapons, we have lost control of our future and of the future generations. I think it is time that the leaders of countries realize we have the right to live and it shouldn't depend on whether or not they decided to shoot off some nuclear weapons. God is our leader. Let Him be in control of everything.

Lottery—How come people don't pay any attention to you until you win a lottery?

Loudspeaker—I's not how loud you talk that will make people listen, it's how you convey your message with a human touch that they can feel in their hearts.

Lounge—Why do some companies make the rest rooms for women fancier than those for men? Don't they realize men like to sit in chairs and lie down on couches, too?

Love Child—A gift from God no matter how you slice it.

Love Seat—After a divorce, this becomes a dust collector in the attic.

Low—It's all right to lay low sometimes, but don't let it become a habit.

Low-key—It's okay to talk lowkey as long as your actions are high-keyed.

Lucifer—He can make the scalp of a bald man curl.

Luck—Don't depend luck when hard work will ensure the results you want.

Luggage—If you arrive safely at an airport, don't complain if your luggage is lost. Better your luggage lost than you.

Lukewarm—Total commitment is needed to achieve something in life, so don't approach anything halfway and then quit.

Lumberjack—Appreciate them, because they risk their necks to cut down the timber needed for your dream house of tomorrow.

Luncheonette—Not as big as a restaurant, but their cozy feeling can't be matched.

Lure—Don't be lured unless you know what awaits you.

Lust—It's all right to lust for something, but don't let this desire be fulfilled if you know its wrong.

Luxury—To live in a free country. It doesn't come any better.

Lyricist—They write the songs that ease your tension and send you into a smooth-sailing feeling.

Mace—If the occasion arises, for you to use this, God forbid, give it the chance to defend you by learning how to use it properly.

Machine—Work hard, but don't become like a machine. Machines can't love, but you can love and you need to take time out for your feelings once in a while.

Macho—This word should be banned from the English language. What a stupid way to judge a man, whether he's macho or not. The world would be a better place with a wimp with a heart of gold than a macho man with ice water in his veins.

Mad Money—Money put aside so you can afford to act crazy once in a while.

Magazine—Read the right kind of magazines and learn from them, and maybe someday you can write for one or publish your own.

Magic—Beautiful to learn and entertain others with.

Magnetism—Let your mind be like a magnet, picking up and storing what is needed for you to be the person you want.

Mailman—Keep Fido under control when he comes, otherwise you may wind up getting your own mail.

Malice—Don't create anymore evil in the world than there is already.

Malignant—If you have a growth that is malignant, keep up your spirits and know you are not alone. You are part of the in crowd, the in crowd of courageous people who will help.

Man—Why some men use the term, "I want to have a man-to-man talk with you," I don't understand. People talk with each other every day. Is this macho talk or what? Two men talking who don't fit this image, what kind of talk are they having? A wimp-to-wimp talk?

Ma-about-town—It's all right to be a man-about-town as long as you don't have a bunch of kids-about-town.

Maneuver—Maneuver your way to the top, then help those down below make it to the top, too.

Man of the house—Sometimes the woman of the house can be just as effective at running a house and making a perpetrator head for the hills. So don't judge strength by gender.

Manhole—This is the closest thing some people get to having a home.

Mannequin—Make sure you show enough life so that people don't mistake you for a mannequin.

Mantel—May your mantel reflect what is good about life, not what is bad.

Manure—Never knock what's under you, because you wouldn't want it above you.

Manuscript—May the manuscript of your life read like a Bible.

Marathon—Whether you are in a marathon or marching to your own tune, just keep doing it, for exercise is the best policy.

March—Even though you may experience problems in your life, be like the song "Onward Christian Soldiers" and march on.

Marching Orders—If you are facing a wife bigger than you with a frying pan, I would say, "March."

Margin—Be sure when you provide for the needy, it is by a wide margin.

Marijuana—This is not legal to take but drinking in a bar is, which could lead to a car accident if you had too much to drink. Somebody could get hurt and even killed. Is taking marijuana more dangerous than drinking too much? In some cases marijuana is a lifesaver, because some people take it for medical purposes.

Marines—God bless them, because they are what being brave is all about.

Mark—Make sure the mark you leave in life betters the quality of life for all and isn't easily erased.

Market—If the stock market falls, don't feel bad about it if you have your health. If you are healthy, you own the best blue chip stock in the world.

Marriage—When a couple wants to spend their lives together, with their love for each other being their guide as they journey through life.

Marriage of Convenience—Not a convenience if your partner has bad breath, is homely, or if your mother-in-law falls in love with your spare bedroom.

Mars—If the planet is as good as the Mars candy bar tastes, attempts to go there are well worth the effort.

Marshal—Their courage and strength can mean the difference between life and death for the victims of crime.

Martyr—May they be blessed forever because of the sacrifice they made for a cause.

Mascot—Sometimes you can't tell the difference between the mascot and some of the people in the crowd at a game.

Masculine—Don't worry if you are a man and people think you act a little bit feminine or if you are a woman and you act a little bit masculine. If you are comfortable with yourself, the hell what people think.

Mask—Wear one at Halloween, but don't hide behind one the rest of your life.

Masquerade—Don't try to fool those dear to your heart, because those once fooled aren't likely to be as dear towards you as before.

Massage—It's all in the hands, and let's hope it stays there, otherwise can an affair be far away?

Mastectomy—This doesn't have to make you feel different, because you control how you react to something, and so make an effort to feel good about yourself. Your body doesn't make you a person, you make yourself person by the feelings you have about yourself inside.

Master of Ceremonies—We are all the master of ceremonies of our own lives, so do yourself a favor, and enjoy yourself.

Master's Degree—Don't worry if you don't have one. Being yourself to the best of your ability is your master's degree.

Matador—A wrong move and this person could have his sex life altered for a little while.

Matchmaker—Don't match people unless you are willing to take responsibility for your failures, too.

Maternal—A good mother should be appreciated and rewarded with the love she deserves.

Mathematics—Learn this well, because the more you use your head, the less the dust balls will accumulate.

Matinee—A matinee performance is just as good as an evening one, because the performers are more relaxed.

Mattress—Nowadays if you watch television, listen to the radio, or read the paper, you get the message: Don't smoke, don't drink, be careful with your sex life, and watch what you eat. About the only safe thing to do is lie naked on a waveless waterbed with an oxygen mask on.

McCoy—It's wonderful if you can afford the real McCoy, but some people can't.

Meadow—Protect the meadows, because we need them for the peace and quiet they inspire.

Mean—Don't be mean when kindness is so much better.

Measure—Don't measure people by their faults. Strengths are better to judge people by.

Mechanic—A good one can turn a lemon into a peach of a car.

Medal—Not everybody receives a medal when he or she performs a good deed. Some people go through life doing good for others without getting recognized for it. For their recognition is not of this world but next.

Meddle—Do this only when it will save somebody or something from harm.

Medicaid, Medicare—Let's hope the federal government keeps these programs going, because there are some people who really need the help.

Medicine—Take your medicine when you are sick, because years of hard work went into learning how to mix the right prescription for you and everybody else.

Medicine Man—Some of the medicine men from years ago could have done more for a person today than some of the quacks running around today.

Megaphone—A loud and strong voice, just as if you were using a megaphone, is needed sometimes to get your message across.

Member—Try to be a member in good standing of the human race.

Memento—It is nice to buy a souvenir when you are on a trip, but what you see with your own eyes will last longer, and it doesn't cost you anything but your memory.

Memorial Day—A beautiful day to remember those loved ones who have gone before us. They have paved the way so that we don't have to be afraid to die.

Mend—You can mend a broken heart, but what can you do for a broken mind?

Mental Health—Some people hold it against you if you run for public office and you've had a nervous breakdown or shock treatments. But look at some of the people in office. When they leave office, some of them could use shock treatments.

Mentor—The greatest mentor there was, was Jesus Christ, because He taught how you can overcome a cross and be whole again.

Mercy—Have mercy when it is needed to straighten out a crooked heart.

Mermaid—If you see one, take a swim with her and you will have a good fish tale to tell your wife.

Merry-go-round—Every community should have a merry-go-round. To me it means joy and peace. It's the symbol of the good things in life.

Messenger—Let's hope there is a message of peace from every country of the world everyday of the week.

Microphone—Most people use this to give a speech. Give your speech with emotion and conviction, otherwise the microphone may be the only thing that doesn't walk out on you.

Microscope—Don't be the kind of person who has to examine everything under a microscope before you accept something as fact.

Microwave—Nice to cook in, but it doesn't beat food cooked the old-fashioned way.

Middle Age—When you have a roll around your stomach for every year of your life.

Middle Class—The heart of America. The bridge between rich and poor. We must remain strong, because for America to survive, we must survive. So let's hope and pray we do.

Midshipman—They serve on water so we can enjoy peace of land.

Mile—Some people suffer such hardships in life that you'd be lucky if you were able to walk a block in their shoes, let alone a mile.

Milestone—For some people, it's everyday they make it through the night.

Military—They enable the freedom eagle of America to fly high and mighty and proud.

Milk—Make a cow happy and drink milk for a healthier you.

Milkman—Don't fool around with the milkman, otherwise his truckload of milk might turn into frozen yogurt, especially in the wintertime.

Milky Way—A nice way to relax at night is to look up at the Milky Way in the sky or eat a Milky Way candy bar.

Mill—People who work in a mill of any type know what hard work is all about.

Millionaire—You don't have to be a millionaire to enjoy the best things in life, like the sun, stars, etc.

Millions—The term millions is used for describing how many people watch an event or TV program. But remember, every one of those people is a somebody. Nobody lives in obscurity. God knows every one of his children and where they are. So the next time you hear the word celebrity, look in the mirror and see if for yourself. In God's world you are one.

Mind—You hang up a picture because it brings happiness for you and for other people. So let your frame of mind be one that brings happiness for you and for other people.

Mind-blowing—When a politician gives a straight answer.

Mind Reading—If everybody had this power, people would be afraid to think. Thank goodness for the secrets in the mind as long as only good thoughts are programmed into action.

Minefield—Don't let the minefields of life distract you from your goals in life.

Minesweeper—To operate one of these is an important job, because you are clearing the way for the progress of the world.

Minimum Wage—Everyone should get a just wage to enable them to buy the necessities of life and also save some.

Miniskirt—The skirt that made the sidewalk move.

Minister—A good one will give you peace for your troubled soul.

Mink—Remember where it came from, and you wouldn't wear it as often.

Minor—Important that the right guidance is given to this person for his or her development into adulthood. If this is your responsibility, be sure you are up to the task at hand.

Minuteman—If all workers in the USA were like this as far as work goes, ready to work in a minute's notice, all the goods manufactured in the USA would last more than a minute.

Miracle—When the power of God takes over when human hope is gone.

Mirror—Don't let this be your downfall in the morning. It's what you think of yourself as a person that counts, not what image a mirror reflects back to you in the morning in silence.

Miscarriage—Don't despair; have your own private angel in heaven.

Mischief—Devore more of your time to charity work, and your time for mischief will be in for some idle days.

Misery—Learn the misery others go through, and you will better understand their fate.

Missile—Let's hope the guided missile systems of all countries of the world become so deteriorated from not being used that they almost need a Seeing Eye dog to guide them.

Missing Link—What worries me is: if they find the missing link, will they know what to connect it to?

Missionary—They brave the unknown so our lives become more enlightened.

Mistletoe—Be careful where you hang this. The person who kisses you, maybe won't exactly be your heart's content.

Mistress—Why divide your love, when devoting all your love to your wife would be more productive for your marriage?

Misunderstanding—Don't let a misunderstanding ruin your relationship with another person. Life is too precious to be wasted because of actions done or words spoken.

Mob—A lot of animals behave better in a group than a lot of people do.

Model—Just because you aren't on a magazine cover doesn't mean you're not pretty enough to be a model. Magazine covers are tomorrow's garbage. You are today's news, starring as yourself.

Molasses—To be slower than molasses in January isn't so bad, just so you pick up some speed by July.

Mold—God made you from a mold that wasn't repeated, because he wanted you to be you. Nobody can be you better than you can.

Molotov Cocktail—If you drink too much, you can become one of these: a time bomb waiting to go off.

Moment—Every moment is precious in your life, so learn to use them wisely.

Monday—Behind every weekend is a Monday. Remember that when you wish the weekend to come.

Money—Some see green. Others see the love for their fellowmen that money can't buy.

Monk—God bless them, because they pray for us so that we can enjoy the world they gave up.

Monkey—A monkey on your back is better than having an ape on your back.

Monocle—Wear one if that's your thing. In life you should do your things as long as you don't hurt anybody or anything by doing it.

Monopoly—Own all the commodities you want; you still can't take it with you.

Monorail—Support one for your area, because the sooner we eliminate pollution the better.

Monster—Some children act like monsters. If you would see the examples set by their parents, you would know why.

Montessori Method—A beautiful method to teach children how to act on their own dreams.

Monument—Most of the people who do the most good in life aren't rewarded after they are gone with monuments built in their memory. A monument will fade, but the memories of the good deeds done by the people will go on forever, and at least good deeds don't have to be pigeon-proofed.

Mood—Remember when you're feeling blue, it will pass because as time passes so will your mood.

Moonshine—The shine that lit up the countryside and gave the city lights a run for their money.

Mop—Don't let your hair look so bad that people will want to tip you upside down and use you as a mop.

Moral—Do what is morally right in life, and you will do all right.

Morality—When all the countries of the world treat all mankind equal, you will see the moral value of the world go up to a new record high.

Morning—Bring cheer to people at the beginning of the day, and at night you will be satisfied you did your best.

Morse Code—Some people use such highfalutin' words when they talk, you would think they were talking in Morse code.

Mortarboard—Your graduation may have seemed like a breeze, but beware of the real world. It is well-rounded, so you have no corner to hide in. Be prepared to represent yourself, because the audience is waiting for you, whether you are ready or not.

Mortician—One job where you won't get any backtalk, and if you do, the person wasn't as stiff as you thought.

Mosquito—This is the state bird of some states.

Mother Superior—She is the guide for those girls or women who want a way of life outside of the world without leaving the inside of the world.

Mother Tongue—Don't forget your mother tongue when speaking another language, because your roots are the foundation that talk the loudest.

Motion Picture—Give support to the clean family pictures, and maybe the bad ones will disappear.

Motorbike—Drive carefully on this, otherwise your style might be a motorized wheelchair.

Mountaineer—They obtain the top that we dream of.

Mousetrap—They say build a better mousetrap and the world will beat a path to your door. That may be true, but your lawn will look like hell.

Mouth-to-mouth Resuscitation—Watch it to learn, use it to save, and pass it on for the survival of others.

Mouthwash—Some people should use it to save the world from extinction.

Mule—Don't knock a mule, because you may be married to a worse jackass.

Multicolored—The human race is multicolored but under the same power source: God.

Multiple Sclerosis—It tries to cripple you physically but it never can handicap your spirit if you don't let it.

Mumbo Jumbo—Congress in session.

Murder—Never take a life unless somebody is trying to take yours.

Muscle—You don't need big muscles to help people in need.

Muscular Dystrophy—Look around the corner, the cure is coming around the bend. Keep your spirits high and reach for the sky, and you will know dreams do come true.

Music—Practise it, and someday you will provide the music people want to hear.

Musical Chairs—A good game to play with other people if your wait gets to be too long in the waiting room of a doctor's office. Of course, you might have to wake up some of the other people in the waiting room before you can start.

Music box—One of the greatest joys in life is a music box. Wind one up and play it to your heart's content.

Mystery—Let your life be a mystery and let it be up to you to solve it. That way you will never get bored with yourself.

Nag—Don't nag anybody, because life is hard enough without you making it even harder for somebody.

Nail—Nail down your goals in life, act upon them, and see them become a reality.

Nail Polish—Some of the most beautiful paintings in the world are not hanging on walls, but on fingernails.

Naked Eye—Take care of your eyes, and you will have something more valuable than any optical instrument.

Name—No matter what your name is, the person you want to be.

Namesake—Same name, different people, but hopefully the same spirit to live life to the fullest and to do themselves proud for country and mankind.

Nanny Goat—Get a goat, for cansake.

Nap—The difference between a tired mind and a more productive mind is this.

Napkin—Don't let grease beat a path to your door, use a napkin.

Narrow-minded—Don't let other people's narrow-minded views keep you from a broad-minded outlook on life.

National Debt—Is it any wonder people have charge account debt? Look at our government, which is more in debt and continues to spend. Only when a country sets the right example, will its citizens follow suit.

National Guard—Thank them for being on alert for our protection.

National Parks—Take care of them, because their beauty and the enjoyment they provide for mankind is too valuable to lose.

Natural—Be natural, because you never can tell who is watching.

Natural History—Learn it and let it be a showcase of your mind.

Nature—Take care of it, and it will take care of you in return.

Naughty—It's okay to have fun once in a while, but keep it clean.

Nazi—Hitler thought he could kill off a race, but their ideas and principles will live on forever.

Near—Appreciate your loved ones when they are near, because when they are far away, you will know the difference.

Necktie—Some men wear a certain tie to make a statement, which some other men are making a book with their choice of a tie.

Needle—If your life feels like a needle in a haystack, maybe it's time to get a beeper for your needle.

Needlepoint—A beautiful skill to learn and a beautiful way to preserve the beauty of life.

Neighbor—Try to get along with your neighbors. You never can tell when their helping hands will be needed by you.

Nerve-racking—Having diarrhea on a stalled elevator or having a shot given by a cross-eyed nurse.

Nervous—Get help if your nerves interfere with your life.

Nest—A nest is meant to leave, but don't forget how it was when you are gone.

Nest Egg—Shop and spend wisely, and your golden years truly will be golden.

Network—If you believe what all the network news tells you, then you believe that politicians never lie.

Newspaper—Read it, but don't swallow it all.

New Year's Day—The first day of the new year won't make a difference in your life unless you decide to change it yourself.

Next—If you would turn all your next 'times' into now 'times', the right times for accomplishing something would become a part of your life.

Nice—Be nice, because a cheerful world is better than a crabby one.

Nightcap—Be sure your nightcap isn't so strong that it caps your morning.

Nightclub—It doesn't hurt to go into a nightclub once in a while, as long as you don't drink too much, the music isn't too loud, and rowdiness doesn't reign supreme.

Nightmare—Don' let nightmares dictate your life. Get help if they keep occurring.

Night School—This gave education a shot in the arm, because it gives everybody the chance to learn.

Nobel Peace Prize—A beautiful prize because it encourages peace throughout the world.

Noise—A party is all right, but show some concern for your neighbors and cut down on the noise.

No Man's Land—Don't knock it, because it could be the next Walt Disney World.

Nonfiction—Everybody's life starts out this way, but some people use fiction to squirm their way out of tight spots.

Nonstop—Go nonstop when it comes to overwhelming despair and replacing it with hope.

Noodle—For duck soup use your noodle.

Noon—So what if you have to brown-bag it? At least you have some food to put in a bag; some people have nothing at all.

Normal—There's nothing wrong with being normal but being different doesn't hurt. To accomplish something in life, you have to stand out from the crowd, so be prepared to march to your own drummer. You may be laughed at, but your accomplishments will silence those laughs forever.

Northern Ireland—The people fighting in Northern Ireland are supposed to be Catholics and Protestants, but they are not. Catholics and Protestants who practise their don't act this way.

Nose Job—For a nosy person (one who doesn't mind his or her own business) it's like capping a gusher.

Note—Play an instrument if it will cheer somebody up, including yourself.

Notebook—For a couple not talking to each other buy them a notebook.

Nothing—Everybody and everything is something.

Notice—Notice your surroundings and be pleasant with those around you.

Notorious—Better to be one of God's little children than one of Satan's biggest you.

Novel—You may not have the talent to write a novel, but living one's life takes more talent.

Now—Now is the time to change your ways if you are causing harm to others.

Numb—Don't be out of action too long, the world needs you.

Nun—A beautiful vocation because of the sunshine they bring to others.

Nuptials—Say the right kind of nuptials: the everlasting kind.

Nurse—They can make a difference in your recovery from your illness. Remember to thank them before you leave the hospital.

Nursery—**Spend all the money you want on a nursery,** but in the end it is the love you provide a child that is priceless.

Nurseryman—He keeps America green and smelling fresh, so do your part, too, to keep the trend going by taking care of the plants and trees you buy from him.

Nursery School—Sometimes things taught to a child at home in the early years exceed those things at pre-school.

Nursing Home—It's crazy when you think in kindergarten the kids take naps, while at the nursing homes they have the patients playing contact football. (It seems like this anyway.) Who needs the rest more?

Nurture—Nurture yourself to the highest level of life and live your life as only you can live it.

Nutritionist—They look out for the stomachs of the world, so stomach them the best you know how with the foods they recommend.

Nutshell—Some people can sum up their speeches in a nutshell, for some other people it's more like a band shell.

Oarsman—They practise hard, and whether they win or not, they deserve all the applause they get.

Oath—Don't get in the habit of making promises you can't keep.

Obedient—Obedience is hard sometimes, but people will remember you for it.

Obituary—Don't let anybody write you off. You may be dead to the world, but your soul lives on.

Obligation—You have the obligation to be yourself to the best of your ability, so pick up your feet and march on.

Oblivion—You won't be forgot ten if you leave behind mindful impressions of yourself.

Obscure—Nobody is obscure in God's world.

Observant—Be observant to your surroundings, and you might be the link to a crime solved.

Obsolete—If you don't develop you mind, your mind will become this.

Obstacle—An obstacle can be removed if you make up your mind nothing is going to bother you.

Occasion—Take the occasion and say 'thank you' to someone who deserves the credit for what he or she did for your life.

Ocean—Enjoy it if you are near it. If not, think of the nearest lake, river, or pond as your ocean.

Oceanography—Support it, because water is a commodity that should be preserved to its fullest potential.

Ocelot—Preserve them, because any spots in the darkness of the wild are better than spots in the lights of the city.

Octogenarian—You can enjoy life no matter what age you are. Never look at yourself as a burden to society because of your age. You are an asset to society, because you bring to the world your experience at living.

Odd—There is beauty in difference. There is nothing odd about it.

Off—Make wise investments, and your nest egg will enable you to take off and enjoy your retirement early.

Off Broadway—Some plays off Broadway provide more laughs for people with problems than some on Broadway.

Office—Just because you don't have an office doesn't mean your job isn't important. It is a good thing some people have their own office because then you don't have to look at them.

Officeholder—Be sure it's just your office you hold and not excess money from lobbyists for favors granted.

Off-limits—Make your home off-limits to those teenagers who have a bad influence on your children. Don't let your good example go up in smoke because you gave in to your children and their peers.

Off the Record—Be careful of what you say. What you consider off the record may become "see you in court."

Off the Street—Once in a political convention after presidential candidate was picked, a man came off the street and said he wanted to be the vice presidential candidate. A lot of people laughed because they thought of him as just an ordinary citizen. Nobody is ordinary. Everybody is special in his or her own way. This person could have done just as good a job as any of them or even better.

Oil Field—Save your money, because when they dry up you can't pocket air.

Oil painting—Learn it and preserve the beauty of life on canvas.

Old-fashioned—What some people consider old-fashioned is just good common sense.

Old Maid—She may be unmarried, but at least she doesn't have to answer to anybody.

Old Testament—Read it and then read the New Testament, and the life of Christ will become real before your eyes.

Old-timer—It takes an old-timer to clear the path for the newcomers, so don't think of age as a liability. It is a gift to have a lifetime of experience to your credit.

Old Wives' Tale—How come they call it old wives' tale? Don't old husbands gossip, too?

Olympics—Bring back the sportsmanship and forget about the standings of the countries

One—They say everybody's vote counts, but you know if one person wins an election by only one vote, the losing person is going to ask for a recount. Doesn't the one vote mean anything?

One-horse Town—Never misjudge a one-horse town. Maybe at night everybody lets his or her hair down and it becomes a stampede.

One-upmanship—I's all right to stay one step ahead of competitor as long as you play fair. Don't step up your competition while he or she is down.

Onion—A good eyewash and it's edible.

Open-heart Surgery—The heart is opened and operated on. After the operation, the heart is closed again, but there is now life in a closed heart. Love can flow again.

Open-minded—An open mind progresses, while a closed mind deteriorates.

Opinion—Don't keep your opinion to yourself if it means life or death for somebody.

Opportunity—Take the opportunities that come your way, because opportunities are chances that might never come your way again.

Optician—They have their sights on the world for a better vision for all.

Optimism—If you could bottle this and sell it, you would make a fortune.

Orange—Eat one whenever you can see the fruits of your labor grow. Vitamin C will be your battle cry.

Orangutan—If some people remind you of an ape, you better look at yourself in a mirror. Maybe they resemble some chips of your old block.

Oratory—Practise your speaking, and maybe public speaking won't be a stranger to be frightened of.

Orbit—Some people you wish would go into orbit and find out where they came from and stay there.

Orchestra—Your life should be like an orchestra. During a performance, if an orchestra makes a mistake, they don't quit playing and start over; they keep on playing. That's the way you should be with your life.

Orchid—Buy an orchid for that special someone in your life.

Ordeal—Don't let an ordeal get you down, turn it into a fortunate experience.

Order—Something may be just what the doctor ordered, but when you see the price of it, the doctor should have paid for it, too.

Organist—Their mask can give you the tranquil mind that you are looking for.

Orphan—Love can be the parents they don't have, so let it flow from your heart to theirs.

Oscar—Some of the greatest performances are not on the stage or in the movies. They are given by people who think of, care for, and help other people more than themselves in the movie known as "life."

Ostrich—Don't stick your head in the sand so much to avoid problems that people start calling you the sand bird.

Ouster—Evict the bad thoughts from your mind and let good thoughts filter in your heart, soul, and mind.

Outdoors—Nowadays they build domes to play football, etc. in. Stores have sidewalk sales where all the merchandise is put on the sidewalk. The next thing that is coming is underground travel. You will be driving your car under the roads you used to travel on. Any four-legged creature that comes along will use the roads. When a pedestrian crosses the street, it won't be hit and run anymore, it will be run and bite.

Outfit—Don't wear outfits so outlandish that people are debating whether you are from Mars or bought your clothes from your local army surplus store.

Outgrow—You never outgrow the child in you. It is nothing to be ashamed of, because it was part of you once and still is.

Outhouse—Don't knock it. It may come back into style if your indoor plumbing ever gets clogged.

Out-of-date—Out-of-date things sometimes give you a newer spirit about life than new things do.

Out-of-towner—When an out-of-towner comes to your town, remember to project a good image of you and your town. You are priceless when it comes to playing a part in the tourist trade for your town and state.

Outsider—An outsider may be the breath of fresh air your group needs.

Oven—A baker has it hard in the summertime because an oven is hot. Which a baker has to work around.

Over—Some people you can knock over with a feather, and yet some other people you can't make a dent in them if you hit them over the head with a ton of bricks.

Overalls—Don't be ashamed to wear overalls. They are the symbol of what hard work is all about.

Overcharge—Don't overcharge, because your credit represents you as a human being and you need to give a good account of yourself.

Overdraw—Be careful how you balance your checking account, because if you overdraw your account, the overdraft charge is almost as much as a down payment on a house.

Overhead—The overhead at any company are those people who don't use their heads.

Overlook—Don't forget those people who helped you get where you are today.

Overstay—Don't stay too long in somebody's house that the next time they see you coming, they put up a "Beware of Dog" sign and they don't even have a dog.

Over-the-counter—Be careful of some over-the-counter products. Consume too much of them, and you may end up under-the-counter.

Overtime—Don't live so high off the hog that you need overtime to make ends meet.

Overwork—It's okay to work hard, but don't overdo it so much that six feet under is beginning to look like a welcome relief to you.

Owl—Be wise as an owl, but don't toot your horn all night like one. Party time and job time don't mix. Work your best now, and later on an older and wiser you can party your best.

Own—Be your own self, and you won't have to worry about people getting the wrong impression of you.

Pacemaker—Thank God for the pacemaker. The world needs every heartbeat it can get, because when a heart beats it is capable of spreading love around the world.

Pacifier—Buy one for somebody who sucks, if you know what I mean.

Paddy Wagon—With all the drug use nowadays, the police will have to start using a jumbo 747 to pick up all the suspects instead of a paddy wagon.

Page—Some people's lives are so juicy, you can take just one page out of their life and make a full-length movie out of it. The refund for the dogooders after the movie might be long, but that's beside the point.

Pain—Some people have as much or more pain than other people in this world, but they don't say anything. They suffer quietly.

Pair—It takes two to tango, so remember that when the results are in.

Palace—Your house may not be a palace, but at least you have a roof over your head and you can be just as royal as you want to be.

Pallbearer—If doing this makes you nervous, don't feel bad, you're not alone.

Panda—These are the cutest bears around. Too bad there aren't more around to enjoy.

Pandemonium—Stay cool and don't push the panic button during tension-filled pressure situations in your life.

Pants—Who cares who wears the pants in the family as long as somebody wears them. Isn't it time we quit stereotyping people once and for all?

Pantywaist—A man who you think is a pantywaist may have the strength inside of him to climb the highest mountain in the world. Don't judge a book by its covet.

Paperboy or girl—The real heroes in today's world, especial when the weather is bad.

Paperweight—Some people's heads would do just fine.

Parachute—If your parachute doesn't open on the way down, flap your arms like hell and pray for a miracle.

Paragraph—If you write sentences that sound alive, your paragraphs will make quite a story.

Pardon—Forgive someone when the hurt from not talking to them is greater than the offense.

Parkinson's Disease—A badge of courage to the people who suffer from this disease. They survive by conquering the urge to quit when it's the hardest to live.

Parochial School—Support one and have an input in the results of your child's education.

Parrot—I hope you enjoy your parrot if you have one teach her or him right, and it won't give away any of your trade secrets when you have company. Otherwise you may want to give Polly more than a cracker when your company is gone.

Partake—Be a part of the human race and help develop world peace for all mankind.

Part-time—Don't knock a part time job; it's good experience for your career planning.

Party Line—It's time to get a private line when the party on your line knows more about your sex life than you do.

Passenger—If a back-seat driver gets the best of you, pull over to the side of the road and ask him or her if he or she wants to drive. If he or she doesn't want to drive, tell them it's either a brisk walk or silence is golden. He or she has the choice. Driving is nerve-racking enough nowadays without somebody adding another obstacle to it.

Passport—Make sure you take a good picture, otherwise you might be mistaken for a spy when you travel through a foreign country.

Password—Know the password to your success, and you will gain admission to the rewards you have earned from your hard work.

Patch—Patch up your differences with you conscience and admit to the consequences of your actions. The sooner you pay your dues, the sooner you can get on with your life.

Patience—You need this in a doctor's office. Sometimes by the time they call you in from the waiting room, you can't move, because your feet and legs have fallen asleep.

Patriot—It's okay to love and defend your country as long as you remember God made the whole world.

Patrolman or woman—Be good to them, because their beat is our beat to enjoy because of them.

Pawnshop—Don't pawn any item that has given you more joy than your money problems. Sometimes the retrieval process is too late, and the only thing left for you to retrieve is the memory of the item.

Paycheck—Try to save some money and don't depend on living paycheck to paycheck. If you spend too much money, you might be crying cheek to cheek with your husband or wife.

Payoff—Be careful of a payoff, otherwise you might pay up behind bars.

Peacetime—Help to make peacetime a reality all around the world all the time.

Pedestal—No matter who you put on a pedestal, they are flesh and blood like everybody else, including the president of the United States.

Pedigree—The best pets are those you buy from the heart, not how much green you dish out for one. All animals need love, whether they have a pedigree or not.

Peekaboo—Don't peekaboo in the wrong place, otherwise they might call you black-eyed Fred or Freda.

Pekinese—They do China proud because of the way they look and walk. They were born to be spoiled.

Penguin—Their walk is worth a million smiles.

Peon—There is no such thing as a peon, because everybody is somebody.

Perfect—Try to be perfect, but don't expect to achieve it, because nobody is perfect except God.

Performance—Everyday try to give the best performance of your life possible.

Perfume—Your perfume should delight people, not knock them out.

Period—Don't let your life be a period. Let it be an exclamation point!

Perk—Give your coffee pot some competition and perk up your life.

Persian Cat—Brush and take care of it, because it is a gem to behold.

Persian Lamb—Better to hear lamb go baa-baa than see one swinging across a disco floor on a woman's back.

Person—We each can only be one person, which is sad, because maybe you're like me and you want to be the whole world.

Personal—No matter what is on the national scene on television, your personal life should be important to you and the force which guides you through life.

Personality—Your personality is what leads you down the path of life, so make sure yours is pleasant.

Perspire—Don't perspire so much that they name a lake after you.

Pester—If you want to pester somebody, pester the devil to stay off your back.

Pet—It's all right to be the teacher's pet if the teacher is beautiful or handsome, but if he or she is ugly and has bad breath, you can have her or him.

Pet Rock—Did you hear the joke about the pet rock? A man comes out of his house crying. A neighbor sees him and asks him what is wrong. He replies, "I am upset because I just had to put my pet rock to sleep.

Petroleum—Use it wisely, because once it's gone, it's gone, it's gone forever.

Pheasant—Provide some feed for pheasants in the wintertime, because they provide some of the beauty in nature.

Phobia—Don't let your fear of something limit your life. Life is too short to have a limitation derail your goals.

Photograph—Be the photographer the world is waiting for.

Physical—A good physical every once in a while will keep the undertaker away, and heaven can wait will become reality.

Picket Fence—Take care of your picket fence if you have one. The beautiful things in life should be taken care of.

Picket Line—Strikes are permitted in America, but I think it's terrible when Americans fight Americans.

Picture—Don't be upset by a bad picture of yourself. Your real beauty can't be photographed: your inner self. But you know it's there.

Pies—Pies are good, so permit yourself a slice of one, once in a while.

Pig—I like pigs, especially little ones. A person should buy one for a pet if you live in the country, and let the good oinks roll.

Pilgrim—Thank God for the pilgrims, because their pilgrimage helped form the nation that is the symbol of peace for all mankind.

Pillar—Be the pillar some people need for strength.

Pine—Smell a pine tree and fall in love with life.

Pin money—Pin money is okay as long as it doesn't become sin money.

Pins and Needles—Sew with pins and needles, don't be on pins and needles.

Pioneers—They opened up the way of living you have today. So be thankful and count your blessings, for without them we wouldn't have what we have today.

Pipeline—Be a pipeline for peace and pass it on.

Pistol-whip—People who pistol-whip other people should have to stand behind a donkey that is in a kicking mood.

Pitcher—It is better to watch a pitcher in a baseball game than to drink a pitcher of liquor.

Pits—Sometimes your life can seem like peach grove. In other words, it's the pits.

Pity—It's all right to take pity on somebody, but don't be the contributing factor.

Plain—Nobody is plain. We all possess the beauty of ourselves.

Plan—Develop a plan for your goals in life.

Planetarium—Support one and take your family to one, and you will realize the joy of having fun together as a family.

Planned Parenthood—Love cannot be planned. It comes from the heart, and it doesn't have a number on it.

Plant—Guards are important, because they set the tone for the employees as they enter the plant gates. They should greet everybody with a smile and a friendly hello. The employees should reply back with a smile and a friendly hello, too. This was the employees will have a good start as they begin their workday.

Plants—Take care of your plants, because some plants bring more joy to people than their fellowman does.

Plaque—The greatest awards are not visible. They are engraved in your heart.

Play—When you play a game, remember to play fair and make the game enjoyable for all. If everybody has fun, everybody wins.

Playboy—A playboy should be careful. He might run into a husband who might not be so playful.

Pledge—Pledge to do your best as you journey through life.

Plow—Plow through your work everyday, and you will enjoy relaxing come day's end.

Plug—Keep plugging away everyday, and your efforts will pay off.

Plumber—A good one can't be replaced by Drano.

Pocket—Don't pocket anything that doesn't belong to you.

Point—Point to the highest star in the sky and make it your goal in life to go as high as you can.

Point of No Return—When you find out after you get married that your mother-in-law holds a black belt in karate.

Pole—Some people wouldn't touch something with a ten-foot pole. A giant wouldn't touch something with a hundred-foot pole, and a small person wouldn't touch something with a one-foot pole. But a brave person would use the pole vault into the situation, hook, line, and sinker.

Police—They protect so you can enjoy life as you should. Say a prayer for these brave souls today.

Police Dog—A criminal's worst enemy. Anybody who shoots one should be made to pay for the training of a new one.

Political—My idea of politics is to hold the convention the first day, the campaign the second day, and the election the third day. Make it a three-day affair every one hundred years.

Politician—Somebody who thinks of himself or herself until election time, then they think of everyone else.

Pontiff—May he be the model of goodwill that the Lord wants him to be.

Pony—Be good to a pony, and take care of a pony because the pony you take care of today may be the derby winner of tomorrow.

Pool—The female version of Minnesota Fats is New York Pockets Mama.

Poor—If you have food to eat everyday and a roof over your head, you are not poor.

Pornography—Somebody must like it and buy it. Why else would it be for sale? In order for it to be stopped, there must be no buyers.

Port of Call—Be sure your port of call includes going to church every Sunday.

Positive—Be positive, because nothing is gained by thinking negatively, so chin up and full speed ahead.

Postage—It's getting so cheaper to hand deliver a piece of mail yourself than mail it through the post office.

Pothole—You don't have to go to Arizona to see the Grand Canyon, just look at the roads you drive on.

Pot Roast—Make one for somebody whose heart you want to melt.

Poverty—It's doesn't have to be if we become hands across America for real.

Powder Room—Exercise room for a woman's tongue.

Power—Use the power within you to change the world for a better tomorrow for everyone.

Prairie—Take care of the prairie, otherwise the call of the wild won't be heard for the next generation.

Prairie Schooner—If you had a race between a prairie schooner and some of the cars manufactured today, I wonder what would win?

Pray—Pray when it is the hardest to pray, because those are the times when the depth of your faith shines through.

Pregnant—Many women have a lot of pain when they give birth. But they are not afraid to go through it again, because the joy after is part of their life forever.

Prejudge—Don't prejudge anybody or anything before the evidence is in. Once the evidence is in, slice it up and put it back together your way. Reach your decision the only way you can: your way. You will then be satisfied with the truth.

Preschool—The minute a child is born, they become a preschooler, so parents—teach them good.

Prescription—Buy one of these, and you will know what it's like to be part owner of Fort Knox.

Presidential Press Conference—Where the questions are longer than the Gerrysburg Address and the answers are shorter than a miniskirt.

Press—The press should tell the facts and let the public decide who is lying or telling the truth.

Price War—If products were priced the way they should be, there wouldn't be a need for price wars.

Priest—A hard job, but a rewarding one because of the peace of mind they bring to people.

Private—Three of the most private things in a person's life should be his or her religion, his or her sex life, and his or her political preference, but today they are the most talked about. I don't understand.

Prizefight—Money can't replace damage to the body.

Profanity—Don't use this to make a point, because bad language doesn't further cause, it only diminishes it.

Profession—Be proud of your job no matter what you do for a living. Even if you clean toilets, you are an important person.

Profit—Don't make a profit at the expense of others. Money made through the suffering of others is scar money because of the scars left on the lives of other people and your soul.

Proofread—Everybody is human, so you might see some mistakes in print once in a while.

Proper—Be in the proper frame of mind to make a decision, and you will like the final results of your actions.

Prostitutes—Don't blame the prostitutes for being on the street. If they didn't have customers, they wouldn't be there.

Protect—Protect the children of today, for they are the future of tomorrow.

Protestors—How come some protestors on both sides of an issue get so violent? Can't they at least sit down and agree that both sides are entitled to their opinions and agree to disagree in a peaceful way?

Pry—Don't pry in anybody's business unless it's a matter of life and death.

Pseudonym—Don't get the real one of you mixed up with the fictitious you, because there is a world of difference between the two.

Psychiatrist—They can give you medicine and counsel, but you have to learn how to help yourself.

Public—The hardest job in the world is one where you wait on the public. You never can tell what their mood will be.

Punch Line—Be sure your jokes have a good punch line, otherwise people will think of you as the stale punch line kid.

Punk Rocker—There is a difference between a pet rock and a punk rocker; one you pet and the other you feel like giving a swift kick in the behind once in a while.

Puppet—A puppet show takes more talent than a Broadway show. To keep the interest span of children it takes the patience of a saint.

Purr—Some people may purr like a kitten, but watch out for the swing of their paw.

Pushup—For people out of shape it's like doing a push down.

Pussyfoot—Cold feet are not the answer to your problems. Action in the right direction will solve your problems.

Pyramid—Proof of what humans can do without modern equipment.

Quack—Better to hear this sound from a duck than to seek medical help from a person like this.

Quadruple—Quadruple your efforts in helping those who need your guiding hand.

Quail—Protect nature so they can survive in its surroundings.

Qualm—Your conscience is the safety belt of your mind, so if you have a qualm about something that means your conscience is working.

Quarantine—We should quarantine hardened criminals on an island surrounded by sharks.

Quarterback—Don't be a Monday morning quarterback unless you can play on the field with the big boys.

Quarter Horse—No matter if you own a quarter horse, half a horse, or a whole horse, be kind to the horse in your life.

Queen—With some queens, you would like to stick the crown they have on their head somewhere else.

Queen-sized—If you eat too much, can a king-sized bed be far behind?

Quench—Quench your thirst, but remember to keep your head clear. Too much strong stuff, and you will see pink elephants in hula skirts.

Questionnaire—Secrets from the heart you don't have to reveal, because they are neither questions nor answers. They are feelings.

Quicksand—Life is like quicksand sometimes; you start sinking and you have to fight like hell to stay afloat.

Quiet—Sometimes the quiet of a library is what you need to solve your problems.

Quill—These worked better than some of the pens manufactured today.

Quilt—Some of your greatest memories go into the making of a quilt.

Quip—Cheer somebody up with a quick one.

Quitter—Don't be a quitter before the final results are in. When you stick something out, the strength is there to live with the outcome no matter what.

Quiver—Don't quiver or shiver when you should deliver.

Quiz—Don't feel bad if you do poorly on a quiz. Hang in there and maybe someday you will be the author of one.

Quote—Don't quote anybody too much, because the quote may be out-of-date by the time you repeat it.

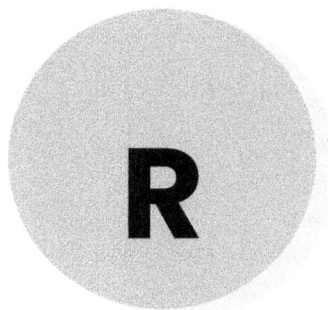

Rabies—Don't forget to get rabies shots for your pets. Don't let others suffer because of your carelessness.

Race Track—Don't let your life be like a race track. Lead your life at your own pace and let other people do the same. Enjoy life, don't race life.

Radical—Don't be too radical, because change must walk the true world its own speed.

Radio—The biggest disappointment with radio is a lot of time you see pictures of the announcers and they don't look like they sound. Maybe it would be beer if you didn't see what they look like and let your imagination run wild on how you think they look.

Raft—A beautiful experience to calm your nerves is to take a raft down a river.

Railroad—Enjoy the railroad, because it is the living history of yesterday, today, and tomorrow.

Rainbow—After the rain comes the rainbow; your life too will have a rainbow after the storm if you just hang on.

Rain Check—Sometimes a rain check on an item turns out to be a tornado hit when you get the item.

Rainwater—Help protect the environment so this will always be the best water there is.

Range—One of the highest ranges in the world is not a mountain. It's the Mormon Tabernacle Choir, and what a beautiful sound it is.

Rape—If this happens to you, find somebody who understands and don't give up until you do.

Rat—Lick poverty, and this won't be a common sight in some people's homes.

Reach—Reach out for a hand and help someone with their journey through life.

Read—Read all you can, for you are America's future.

Ready—Be ready for the roll call on judgment day and hope God knows your name. The impression you make could be the difference between left and right.

Rearview Mirror—There is more action seen in a rear view mirror sometimes than what is seen ahead of you on the highway. A set of eyes in the back of our heads would be the answer for more excitement in our lives. I suppose some people wouldn't be satisfied with that, they would want another mouth. The word motor mouth would be replaced by express train.

Reason—Don't try to find a reason for everything. Live life, don't try to understand it.

Rebate—If products were priced right, you could afford to pay for them and you wouldn't need a rebate.

Reborn—Everyday you acknowledge God, you are reborn in the kingdom of a loving father.

Recite—Look into the mirror everyday and recite that you will be yourself to the best of your ability.

Rectify—Rectify your past, but don't live it.

Redouble—Redouble your efforts to make it a beautiful world for everybody.

Redwood—Thank God for these trees. I hope their beauty lasts forever.

Refine—So what if you are a man who happens to be gentle and refined? You have a great leader to follow. He was gentle and refined too. His name was Jesus Christ. His cross held the greatest strength in the world: Himself.

Reflect—Reflect on the pleasant things of life, and your smile will light up the world.

Refrigerator—Where the pounds jump out at you when you open the door, and it takes no prisoners.

Regard—Send out warm regards to everyone you meet.

Regret—Don't regret anything that can be reversed by a greater effort on your part to do so.

Rehearse—Rehearse your behavior as a human being, and you will be a model for the rest of the world to follow.

Reincarnation—If some people would come back in their true character, the population of jackasses would increase in this world.

Relative—Appreciate them, because you never know when you will need their help.

Release—Release the energy inside you, and the results will be gratifying.

Relief Pitcher—They are asked to build Rome in a day.

Religion—Worship your Lord according to what's in your heart.

Remember—Remember the good times and be thankful. Also, remember to thank the Lord for the roof over your head and for the food on your table.

Repair—Repair a broken heart and let love flow again.

Repay—Repay love rendered with love returned.

Repent—Repent, because if you sinned, you should be sorry.

Report Card—The best mark doesn't appear on a report card: the mark for doing your best despite your grades.

Reptile—Sometimes you can't tell the difference between some of the snakes that crawl on the ground and some of the two-legged kind of the human race.

Rerun—A rerun program on television is sometimes better than the original program. You know more about it the second time around, and you can enjoy it more. Your life is different. Only once around, so make it an original worth living and a memory of you for others to enjoy for years to come.

Reputation—Keep your reputation clean. You're the one who has to live with it.

Research—The more you learn, the more researching your brain goes up and racking your brain goes down.

Resource—Save the resources of nature, because once gone, they are gone forever.

Rest—Rest your eyes once in a while, because your sight is your window to the world and you need a clear vision. Also the world needs a rested you, ready to do your part for mankind.

Restaurant—Find one that serves homemade pies, and you have found one that wants you to feel right at home.

Resurrect—Resurrect the goodness of Jesus in your heart and live it daily.

Retire—Life doesn't make sense sometimes. Some older people have to retire, but they want to keep working. Some younger people have to work, but they want to quit working.

Retreat—Go on a retreat and review yourself as a human being.

Retriever—Take care of your retriever if you have one, because it retrieves the game that lines your stomach.

Return—Return to your roots and feel the soil of your heritage.

Reunion—Don't put up a front when you go for a reunion. You don't have to explain your life to anybody. Live it as you want to, as long as you live and let others live.

Reverse—When you find yourself going in the opposite direction of what you should be going in, just turn around and go back to where you came from. Don't start again until you find the direction with your name on it.

Revive—Give attention to old ideas that would work again for a better life for all.

Rhythm—Appreciate rhythm, because it puts more variety into life.

Rhythm and Blues—Music developed by black Americans, but enjoyed by many people, proof we are all equal. Music doesn't know color. It just knows enjoyment.

Ribbon—Tie a ribbon around the old oak tree anytime you feel like it. You don't have to wait for a special occasion. Whenever it suits you, do it.

Rich and Famous—How come with all the millions of people in the world, only a few are rich and famous? How come just a few people have all the power and are considered the most important people in life, like the president of country? Maybe it's because this has nothing to do with life at all. Life is being yourself to the best of your ability and knowing that God knows who you are and considers you just as important as all the rich, famous, and powerful people in the world.

Rickety—If something of yours is shaky, get it fixed, otherwise you may be the shaky one because of a lawsuit.

Rigger—They have a dangerous job, but a very important one. They are seeing to it that the large parts are moved across a factory floor. The parts have to be hooked up right so the crane can move them. They have to make sure the parts don't slip off the hooks and fall and hurt somebody.

Right—Be right, but admit it when you are wrong.

Ring—Some peoples biggest thrill in life is ringing the bell at a service counter, not once, but many times. Some of them should just tap their head if they like the sound of a bell.

Risk—Take a chance and achieve something worthwhile.

Road—If you take the wrong road, make it the right road by making the necessary changes.

Robin—The symbol of spring arriving, they add color to the rest of the summer. So enjoy it when you see a robin.

Robot—It's all right to own a robot, but if it sasses you, it's time for a program delete.

Rolling Pin—Good protection against a deadly spouse.

Romance—Don't rely on candlelight and music to provide the spark for your romance. You alone should be the spark your love needs.

Rookie—Never underestimate a rookie. Some are more professional than some of the so-called professionals.

Roommate—Be sure you know your roommate before you share a room with somebody. A secret past could become your scary future.

Rope—Don't rope in more than you can handle.

Rose—Nothing can surpass the beauty of the rose. Take care of yourself, and you will have the beauty of the rose.

Rough—Don't worry if you are a woman and you are rough and tough. Be yourself and don't let anybody change you. That is the way you were created, an original work by a creator who doesn't believe in duplication.

Round-the-clock—Don't work round-the-clock unless you like a grave round-the-clock.

Royalty—In God's eyes, all his children are royal.

Rubber Stamp—Be sure to check everything out really well before you give approval to anything, because you may be rubber stamp yourself if the project doesn't work out.

Rumor—Don't let rumors spoil your day. Let a more productive you occupy your day.

Rumpus—Don't cause a rumpus while you are out in public, otherwise you will have your own rumpus room. It is known as the city jail.

Run-down—Don't give up on things that are run-down. Sometimes old is better than new. The way some of the new is made nowadays, it should be run out of the country.

Run-of-the-mill—Nobody is this, because God doesn't make any junk.

Sacrifice—It's all right to make sacrifices, but think of yourself once in a while and don't give the whole store away.

Safeguard—Everybody makes mistakes on the job once in a while. It scares me to think of the people taking care of the nuclear weapons. They are only supposed to shoot them off if they get the order to do so. There are supposed to be safeguards, but it still scares me to think they could shoot them off by mistake.

Sailor—God bless them, because in order to protect America, they are on ships for long periods of time away from their families.

Salvation—Your salvation is in your hands. You choose the route you take, so your destination shouldn't be too much of a surprise to you at the end of your journey.

Sandbox—If you are an adult and you want to play in a sandbox, go ahead. Don't be ashamed of the child in you. You started out as one, don't lose it.

Sanitary Engineers—They collect your garbage, so be kind to them as they make their morning run. If you have an extra big load, help them carry it to their truck.

Satellite Dish—If they add anymore channels on cable, this will have a new name: satellite setting.

Savings Account—Remember your retirement and save. Maybe if you save enough now, you can retire early and let the good times roll.

Scale—Don't jet a scale control your life. Eat properly, and you will have control over yourself.

Scarecrow—It's all right to protect your garden, but don't forget about your home. Have plenty of lightning inside and out. Have someone watch your home when you are on vacation. Above all, trust your police and believe in them. You might find some bad apples in your police force, but overall they protect you and need your support.

Schizophrenia—If you suffer from this, get help.

School—It would be nice if there were an alternative to school for kids who don't like it. Maybe a trade school would better serve their purpose if they are serious about a career goal they have in mind.

Schoolmarm—I think we need to get back to the basics in today's schools. Just as a teacher was known as a schoolmarm years ago, the basics were reading, writing, and arithmetic, and let's add common sense. If you know the basics, you can learn any computer with the greatest computer you have: your mind.

Science Fiction—Some of the people who take drugs look like science fiction. I think life is challenging enough without taking drugs to make it more confusing.

Scientist—They probe the unknown so we can enjoy the known better.

Scooter—Don't drive chis as if you own the road. If you drive one of these too recklessly, you will become part of the road.

Scoutmaster—They lead a troop of Scouts that will be the future of tomorrow. If they guide them right, it will make all the difference in the world. So if you know a good scoutmaster, thank him or her on behalf of the world.

Scrapbook—Save your memories and let your memories lead you away to some restful relaxation.

Screen Test—Everyday of our life we are tested to be ourselves to the best of our ability.

Scripture—Read it, believe it, and live it.

Sculptor—They permit people to see the world through their art. They represent freedom, because they allow their ideas to escape for the freedom of all to enjoy.

Sea—Preserve the sea, because if we don't, we won't be able to see the sea with the greatest of ease as it gets smaller.

Seat Belt—Wear one, because if you don't, you might go flying, and it won't be with the greatest of ease, either.

Second Fiddle—Sometimes second fiddle is the finest fiddle.

Secondhand—If taken care of, it's just as good as new.

Secretary—Don't worry if you can't keep up with the next secretary as far as clothes go. You are there for the quality of your work, not as a fashion plate for the whole world to see.

Secret Service—Their stare can grow hair on a bald man.

Security Blanket—If you have one, don't be ashamed of it; in today's world you need all the security you can get.

Seesaw—If this book seems like a seesaw, it's because life is a select seesaw.

Select—Your life is based on the selections you make, so choose wisely.

Self—The greatest mistake in life you can make is to depend on other people for your happiness. Self-implanted happiness is the greatest happiness of all.

Self-employed—Set an example for others to follow. Show them what one person can do on his or her own.

Self-help—Self-help is the greatest help of all.

Sell—Don't sell your soul to the devil, because nothing on Earth can hold a candle to heaven.

Seminary—Support these before we lose the training ground for our future religious leaders.

Senator—The greatest tax break the American people get is when some of these retire.

Send-off—Give somebody a good send-off when they leave, because before they reach their destination they will probably need it.

Separate—One thing may separate the men from the boys, but another thing maybe only the boys can do.

Seventh Heaven—Be careful if the other shoe drops, then instead of seventh heaven it's eighth hell.

Sex—It should be a private matter for the love of it, but nowadays you find it broadcast on the news for the hell of it.

Sexy—I don't know what they mean on television when they say someone is so sexy. We even have polls in America trying to find out who the sexiest people are. Are they trying to find out who has the most sex or what? They should take another poll finding out who cares.

Shakespeare—Read it and give your mind a break from today's literature.

Shamrock—Ireland's pride and joy can be your pride and joy, too, whether you're Irish or not.

Sharecropper—Let's hope everybody who wants to can own a farm and the only people they have to share it with is their own family.

Sheep—You know you have a drinking problem when you start counting bottles of booze on the wall instead of sheep to get to sleep.

Shelf—Besides the material goodies your shelves hold, make sure you also have the spiritual goodies needed for your ticket to heaven.

Shell—Come out of your shell and come forward and be a part of life.

Shelter—Provide the shelter your family needs to grow up strong and firm in their beliefs.

Shepherd—Their occupation was represented at our Lord's birth. What greater compliment can you be paid?

Shetland Pony—Preserve them. They are a national treasure. They are loved by adults and children alike.

Ship—Come aboard God's ship. It is beautiful.

Shocker—A politician lost for words.

Shoplifter—Don't shoplift, because when you do, you just make the prices of the products you buy for others and yourself go up higher. We will never be able to afford to buy anything if shoplifters keep stealing.

Shoptalk—Don't let shoptalk spoil your vacation. Think of pleasure, not work.

Shortstop—Don't count him short, because in the long haul, he is capable of making some good plays.

Shoulder—A shoulder to cry on is all some people ask for in this world. Lend your shoulder; it could make all the difference in the world to them.

Show Business—Everybody is in the business. We show ourselves to the world the best we know how everyday of our lives.

Shrub—Beautify America; plant a shrub and take care of it.

Siamese Twins—These beautiful gifts from God represent peace, because their physical appearance is what we all should be doing for peace: work as one unit to achieve it. They are God's special children. They are a class act, and if everybody possessed the special courage they have, what a beautiful world we would have.

Sickbed—Stick by and help your loved ones when they are on a sickbed. Guide them back to be an active member of society again.

Sideline—It's okay to watch from the sidelines, but don't become a permanent fixture there.

Signal—May your signal in life be green always.

Sign Language—Learn the language and come into the world of the deaf. You may think they can't hear or talk, but their form of communication is so strong and beautiful, to them silence is golden. They are not handicapped. People who don't understand them are.

Silent Majority—People who do their jobs every day and aren't in the news. They make America what it is today: great.

Silverware—Some people are so poor, their silverware is their precious fingers.

Simple—Life can be simple: don't complicate it.

Simple-minded—Don't worry if you aren't sophisticated. With some of these so-called sophisticated people, you almost have to have a dictionary to look up what they are talking about.

Single—A vocation that one can be proud of. It doesn't have to mean being alone or being lonely. Your choice can mean a wide-ranging life.

Single Parent—They are a double parents, which means double work for them. Appreciate them for the double duty they are doing for society.

Skateboard—Be careful when you use your skateboard, otherwise you might be carried out on a board, better known as a stretcher.

Skeleton—Get rid of any skeletons in your closet. You never can tell when somebody else will be cleaning your closet.

Skid Row—After you have seen one, you would sooner skip row from now on.

Skim Milk—Drink it if it means a healthier you.

Skinny-dip—It's all right to go skinny-dipping, just be sure when you come out of the water your skinny-dipping is over.

Skunk—Sometimes it's hard to tell the difference between some of the two-legged ones and the four-legged kind.

Sky—As far as your goals in life, remember the sky is the limit, so start reaching.

Skyscraper—Where cleaning the windows is a high expectations job.

Slack—Don't slack off when you get ahead. Store your supplies for a rainy day.

Slander—If slander is your game, be careful a sue may enter your life, and it's not a woman. In other words, if you don't like paying out money, don't slander.

Slapstick—Clean comedy, not the dirty kind like today.

Sleeping Bag—A lot of poor people have one of these, but it's called sleeping ground.

Sleepy—Be sure you're not sleepy when driving, otherwise your rest stop won't be so comfortable: the ditch.

Slingshot—Years ago kids were satisfied playing with their slingshots, now for some them, a handgun is more their style.

Slogan—Let your slogan be: be yourself to the best of your ability.

Slot Machine—To win at a slot machine, you need the patience of a saint and under-your-breath language.

Slumlord—If some landlords would take care of their property, some people wouldn't have to live in a slum. They could disco in their condo.

Smear—Don't smear anybody or anything. The cleaning-up process may be difficult.

Smelling Salts—We will all have to use this if Satan ever changes his ways.

Smock—Wear one to protect your clothes at work. Some places of work are so dirty, you are almost better off to wear the color black. Some of these places are known as offices.

Smoke—If you like your lungs, don't smoke in excess.

Smoker—Be sure the grass you grow is the kind you cut with a lawn mower and not the kind you smoke.

Smorgasbord—Life is like a smorgasbord. You are not going to like everything that's on the table, including the people you meet. The object, though, is to cry to get along with everybody. Life is too short, so don't spend a lifetime disliking your fellowmen.

Snake—I don't know which are worse, the snakes that crawl on the ground or the kind that have two legs.

Snow—Every household in the snowbelt should have electric driveway. Otherwise, can achy-breaky back be faraway?

Snowball—A snowball in July doesn't have much chance of surviving. You won't have much of a chance at life, either, if you drink too much, smoke too much, or have a loose sex life.

Society—Tries to dictate how an everybody should be and live. God made the world for everybody, so what may be different in society's eyes may be one individual's cup of tea.

Soft—Don't feel bad if you are a man and you have soft and tender hands. Some men are talented at hard labor, while some other men are talented at office work. Just be thankful for what you can do.

Soil—Take care of the soil beneath you, because it's the provider of the food you survive on.

Solar System—What a beautiful proof that there is a God.

Solid—Be solid where your support is needed and wanted.

Sombrero—Wear one for the fun of it and the sport of it. Lastly, wear one if you feel like doing it, because it's your life. Show your style the way you want to.

Sometimes—My heart goes out to couples who adopt a child and a year later or so the natural parents want the child back. Sometimes the courts award the child back to the natural parents. Talk about heartache in a grand style for the adoptive parents.

Son—A lot of fathers want sons to carry on their name or follow in their footsteps. Don't they realize a daughter could do just as good of a job?

Songwriter—They make an important contribution to society, because a lot of them write songs to eliminate some of the sorrow in the world.

Sound—Sound off when somebody is in trouble.

Sound Bites—They call the commercials the politicians make at election time sound bites. What they should be called is "hit you in the pocketbook when the election is over."

Souvenir—Don't take too many souvenirs when staying at a hotel or motel, because the next time you take a vacation, they might not be there. The reason being, they went broke.

Space—Man goes into space, but I think we should feed the hungry and provide shelter for the homeless down here first.

Space Walk—Some people space walk, and they don't even leave earth.

Spare Tire—When it comes to a car, this is almost the whole ball of wax. When you have a flat, without a spare your plans go flat, too.

Sparkle—Let the sparkle in your eyes be the lighthouse for others to travel home by.

Sparrow—God's eyes are on the sparrow, so he is watching you, too.

Special—Everybody is special.

Specialty—Make your specialty being yourself and do the best job you know how.

Speed—Don't speed while driving a car and take away the chance at life of others.

Speedboat—Drive carefully with a speedboat. Don't become a cut-a-canoe-in-half person or tip a boat over for the fun of it fool. The highways have enough speeding jokers on them without turning the waterways into race tracks, too.

Spirit—May your spirit soar as high as an eagle when you wake up in the morning.

Spokesperson—Represent your company well, and maybe someday, instead of being the spokesperson, you will be the company.

Spring Fever—Be careful that this doesn't happen too soon, otherwise you may end up sick from not wearing enough clothes.

Squad Car—Carrier of our protectors, so respect it.

Square—People may think you are square, but maybe you have some of the same ideas that this nation founded on.

Stage—All the world is a stage with everyone on earth playing a part. Some do good, while some others need to try harder. When you don't do your best, you don't become your best.

Stall—If your car stalls on the highway and it is too far and too cold to go for help, wait for the highway patrol. They are God's protectors of the highway. Respect them for the beautiful work they do.

Stamp—It's getting so expensive to mail a letter that in years to come your postal stamps will be known as your diamond collection.

Stars and Stripes—Respect the stars and stripes, because those who fought and died for it did.

Starve—Nobody should have to starve. The food that is wasted in the world everyday would be sufficient to feed everybody in the world.

Statue—Pigeon heaven.

Step—Step in tune to your music, not somebody else's beat.

Stereotype—What sex a person is born doesn't mean he or she will always be that sex one hundred percent emotionally, so don't make fun of anybody.

Stillborn—Hard on the parents, but still a child of God to be enjoyed in memory.

Stockbroker—You have to have steady nerves to do this job, because you are dealing with the ups and downs of somebody else's money.

Stone Age—If you look at the expressions on some people's faces, you would swear the stone age is still going on.

Stool Pigeon—Sometimes for a better world, their courage is the only thing that will pull it off, so don't condemn them when praise is more suitable for them.

Stopwatch—Don't watch the clock, because when you are a prisoner of time, your life is set on time instead of on life.

Storekeeper—Anytime you deal with the public it is a hard job. What makes it hard is you are dealing with people's moods. Some are crabby and some are happy. Then there are those who are in between; you never know which way their mood will swing.

Storyteller—They tell stories that promote happiness around the world.

Stranger—Not all strangers are bad, because after you ger to know them, some become your best friends.

Strength—The strength you build within is stronger than even Hercules could muster.

Strike-out—Don't worry about a strike-out, because you will get another chance the next time at bat. Going down swinging is better than standing like a mannequin and wondering what time of the day it is.

Strong-arm—Don't use strongarm tactics unless you like dentures for a change of pace.

Student—Be a student that a teacher would be proud to have.

Style—If something is cramping your style, maybe you need a new style.

Suffer—Remember when you have pain that Jesus Christ went before you. He knows your cross, because He invented it and He was the first one to test it out. His shoulder is your shoulder to lean on in time of need. You will make it through the night with Christ leading the way.

Suggest—Speak up and let your ideas be heard.

Suicide—May they find the peace they are looking for.

Suitcase—People go on trips to get away from it all but sometimes the thing that is bothering them the most they take along: themselves.

Sunday—God's day, and let's keep it that way.

Sunflower—Grow some to make life more sunny for people to enjoy.

Sunglasses—They help keep the sun out of your eyes and help give you security when you want to be left alone.

Sunlight—Be the sunshine people are looking for.

Sunrise, Sunset—Double proof there is a God.

Suntan—What I don't understand why some people who want a suntan in order to look darker are some of the same people who are prejudiced against black people.

Superman—How can he fly with such tight pants on? You would think he would suffocate his legs.

Superstar—Be the superstar of your life, and you will have your own built-in hero.

Sure—Be sure of yourself as a human being, and people will respect you as one.

Surfboard—People are getting healthier and living longer. Granny even surfboards now.

Survey—They should take a survey of how many people like surveys. The end result could be no more surveys, thank God.

Swan Song—The last call, but it could be your best call, if you make up your mind to make it that.

Swear—Don't swear so much that people try to avoid you like the plague.

Sweepstakes—Win one of these, and you will have more friends than there are people in the world.

Swing—If somebody says when you walk that they would like to buy your swing for their porch, tell them they couldn't afford it.

Symphony Orchestra—Support the orchestra in your area, because they are music to your ears.

Syrup—Some people are like syrup; they stick around too long.

System—If you don't like the way something is done in your community, take an interest in your community, and see if some changes are possible, if not, at least you tried.

Table—It's all right to lay all your cards on the table, just be sure they're played at the right time. Otherwise the deck will be stacked against you.

Taboo—The more you talk and learn about a subject, the less taboo it becomes.

Tailgate—Don't tailgate too close unless you like being part of a double-decker car.

Take—It's all right if people say you take the cake once in a while, as long as you like the cake and don't eat too much in one sitting.

Talk—So what if people think you talk funny, at least the words come out of your mouth.

Tan—Don't feel bad if you have fair skin, dark hair, and don't tan easily and people think you are sickly-looking, God loves you, because that is the way he created you.

Tardy—Don't be late for anything if you can help it. It isn't worth being late because of the knowledge you miss.

Taste Bud—Be sure your taste buds don't get too far out of control that when people see you coming, they say, "Here comes fat bud."

Tattletale—You don't have to worry about a tattletale if you don't do anything wrong for them to tattle about.

Taxidermist—They stuff and preserve our memories.

Teacher—They teach America's future. Pay them wages they deserve. Without them, there is no future to count on.

Team—On a football team, the quarterback gets all the attention. But if the other players weren't on the field with him, he would be out there all by himself. What could he do all alone on the field by himself?

Tear Gas—Used to disperse a crowd, but it can't disperse the cause of the people pro-testing.

Teenager—A hard trip for some, but you will survive because path has been cleared for the you by the teenagers who are adults now.

Television—Nice to watch for entertainment, but don't let it interfere with your life. Brainpower comes from doing, not watching.

Tell—Don't repeat gossip that will hurt somebody.

Teller—A hard job because you have to be fast and balance out at the end of the day.

Temper—Let your feelings be known before you lose your temper. Bottled-up anger explodes like a volcano sooner or later.

Ten—I hate it when a person is asked to score somebody or something on scale of one to ten, with ten being the highest. God doesn't make any ones. He makes tens. It is what we do with it that makes the difference.

Ten Commandments—Read them, learn them, and live by them.

Ten-gallon Hat—Some people are so proud of themselves that a ten-gallon hat would be too small for their heads. Their heads are more suited for a 747 jumbo jet.

Terrace—Learn to relax on a terrace when your nerves get the best of you. If you don't have a terrace, take a walk. Anything to get your mind on track again.

Textbook—You can't always go by the book, because being practical applies more to what is happening today.

Thanksgiving Day—Everyday should be Thanksgiving Day, because everyday we should be thankful for what the Lord has given us.

Theater-in-the-round—The best theater in the world for an actor. Your talent or your lack of talent is in the open. Either way, it is a learning experience that you can't help but get better from.

Theme—Set a theme for your life and try to accomplish it.

Therapy—Be kind to the therapist as you are put through your paces. They put you back on your feet at the price of theirs.

Third Party—Don't blame a third party for a breakup of a marriage. A strong marriage can withstand a challenge from a third party any time. In other words, a strong foundation can with stand a storm anytime of the year.

Thoroughbred—You don't need thoroughbreds to win races. Just get a horse with good legs and teach him or her the spirit it needs and it will be off and running.

Thoughtful—Be thoughtful, and you will be remembered as a person who cared for your fellowmen.

Throat—You know your throat is hoarse when you can win the Kentucky Derby with it.

Thursday—The day that gets trampled over by people in a hurry for Friday. But it's a survivor, and it can stand on its own and be proud.

Tick-Tack-Toe, Tiddlywinks—Play some fun games when your mind turns too serious for you.

Tidal Wave—Don't let a tidal wave of opinion drown you. Learn to tame the wave to your swimming size.

Tight—Don't wear pants so tight that you can't walk and you have to hop from place to place, and overnight you become America's version of the Australian kangaroo.

Time—Some companies have so many meetings that they have to have a meeting just to find out what time the next meeting is going to be.

Time Clock—Don't feel bad if you have to punch a time clock. At least people will know whether you're coming or going; with some people you don't, and they still get paid for it.

Toaster—Don't knock it. It's the greatest wedding gift of them all. You won't starve it you have a toaster.

Toboggan—Go for a toboggan ride just for hill of it.

Toilet Bowl—Some people make you feel like telling them to stick their head in a toilet bowl and flush it.

Tolerate—Tolerate as much as you can, but don't let anybody or anything take away your dignity as a human being.

Tomorrow—Yesterday is gone and tomorrow does not yet long to us, so live today. I heard that one on television.

Ton—Some things hit you like a ton of bricks. Other things hit you like a piece of cake. But if you are prepared for both, there is no difference.

Tongue—They say a cat has nine lives. That is topped only by people who talk so much, you could say they have nine tongues.

Too—At election time, too many hats in the ring become monkeys running in a circle.

Toothache—When you have a toothache, put your trust in your dentist, and I'm sure your pain will go away. Otherwise, if you have to have the tooth pulled, don't despair, there is always the tooth fairy to cheer you up with some money. In other words, there is gold in them hills.

Toothpaste—Brush your teeth, the way you should, and your smile will have the backup team it needs to survive.

Touch—Touch only when the other person wants to be touched.

Touchdown—Don't settle for a field goal in your life when, with a little extra effort, you could have a touchdown.

Toupee—Some toupees were made to sit on a man's head, others could raise the dead.

Tourist—Don't make them feel like at home, because that is what they are trying to get away from. Instead show them a variety of things. They will then know that different places mean different ways of having fun and relaxing.

Towns—It makes me mad when people on television say their hometown is so many miles away from a major city that everybody knows. Be proud of your hometown and don't mention the other city. Your town can stand on its own two feet.

Toy—Let your children make their own toys, then they will know the value of doing for themselves at an early age.

Tractor—A beautiful symbol of what the American farmer is all about. A good one will work its heart out.

Tradition—To hell with tradition. If you want to make a change in life, go ahead and do it.

Tragedy—Don't let tragic situations stop you from a normal life. Use your energy and turn them around.

Tramp—A tramp is described as one who travels aimlessly about as a vagrant. Sounds to me like a description for a person running for political office.

Trampoline—Get one and jump for the joy of it.

Transform—Transform yourself into the human being you want to be.

Transparent—Make sure if people can see right through you, they like what they see, and if they don't, to hell with them as long as you are satisfied with yourself.

Trap—Don't deny freedom, because being free was meant for all mankind, including the members of the animal kingdom.

Trash—Ordinary people (which there are none because everybody is special in his or her own way) are not allowed to burn their own trash. Yet big companies can pollute like hell. Figure that one out.

Travel—No matter how far you travel, somebody has to keep the home fires burning. So enjoy your trip, but don't forget those who make it possible.

Treadmill—You can survive this. If you can survive yourself, you can survive anything.

Trench—You dig your own trenches in life, so don't complain how deep yours are.

Tricks—Don't play tricks on other people unless you are willing to have the same done to you.

Trim—It's all right to be trim, but don't get so carried away that you are carried away, on a stretcher. that is.

Trip—If you want to go on a trip, see all of your home state first. If you don't appreciate what's in your own backyard, you'll never appreciate the rest of the world either.

Trojan Horse—For a person who has everything, give them a Trojan horse filled with chocolates.

Trombone—If you want people to get out of your way, pick up a trombone and play it.

Troops—Learn to march like the troops, and you will learn what life is all about.

Troublemaker—Don't be a troublemaker unless you like life in the slammer.

Trousers—You don't have to worry about the morning after if you keep your trousers on the night before.

Truce—All countries should agree to a truce, then watch peace do its thing.

True—Be true to your own true love.

Truly—When you sign a letter "yours truly," mean it with your whole heart.

Trumpet—Blow your horn, but at a decent hour, so you don't wake up your neighbors.

Trust—Put trust in the one you love.

Truth—The truth may hurt, but lying may not. But guess which one will set you free.

Try—Try to do your best always.

Tuesday—The calm after the storm of Monday.

Tummy—Don't eat so many goodies that you have more rolls than your local bakery.

Tune—Whistle a tune and be happy.

Turkey—Not all the turkeys in this world are the kind served at Thanksgiving time.

Turkish Bath—It's all right to take a Turkish bath as long as you don't look for dessert afterwards.

Turn—Make the correct turns and you will follow the correct paths.

Turning Point—The turning, point in your life won't knock on your door unless you have your porch light on.

Turtle—Some people are as slow as a turtle, but when they are done, it is a job well done.

Turtleneck—Also known as the hickey hider.

TV Dinner—Now known as the cable dinner. It has sexy potatoes, porno steak, and slinky peas, and for dessert, you get a naked surprise.

Twenty-four-hour Store—God is like a store that is open twenty-four hours a day. You can call on Him day and night for help.

Twinkle—Brighten up your life and watch the stars twinkle at night.

Two-faced—Don't be two-faced, because one face of you is sufficient.

Two-time—Everybody thinks the other side is greener, but they forget it has to be watered and mowed, too.

Two-way—Life is a two-way street. It is for you to travel the good side or the bad side.

Typecasting—Don't typecast anyone. Change is a part of life.

Typist—A person who has to type their fingers to the bone but isn't given enough money to bone up their life with.

Ugly duckling—Nobody has to be ugly. You are only as ugly as you allow yourself to be.

Ukulele—Learn to play one to satisfy the Hawaiian in you.

Ultimatum—Don't issue this unless your reserve is ready for a course of action if the results you want don't come out the way you anticipated.

Umbrella—Provide the protection that other people need to make it through the night.

Umpire—Good ones stick to their guns no matter what.

Umpteen—Sometimes when you say something for the umpteenth time, the last time you say it, you are finally understood. All the times before maybe you didn't make yourself clear.

Unborn—I don't know what is a more powerful issue than the protection of the unborn.

Uncle Sam—He likes to spend other people's money.

Uncle Tom—I don't think this exists today as it did years ago. African Americans are beginning to hold their own and are gaining the respect and dignity God intended for them. In the Bible it says everybody is created equal. There was no color barrier when Christ died on the cross. He represented the rainbow known as the human race.

Undecided—Don't go too long like this, because important decisions will be made without you and you won't get the credit you could have had.

Under—When you are under, can above be far behind?

Underarm—Some people's greatest lethal weapons are their underarms.

Underdog—You may be an underdog going into the game, but when it's over you may be the top dog.

Understudy—Sometimes an understudy is flying better in the wings than the main character on stage.

Under you—Don't worry if somebody pulls the rug from under you; at least you still have the floor for support.

Undress—Be sure you undress only when you are alone or know the eyes that are watching you disrobe. Don't be victimized by strange eyes.

Unicycle—Ride a unicycle for the high of it.

Uniform—Don't be ashamed to wear a uniform, because the uniform means you are capable of doing the job implied by the uniform.

Union—Unions aren't so bad. I just wish some of the members wouldn't get so mean when they go out on strike.

Union Jack—The flag of the country where Liz is the top dog and everybody else is a hush puppy.

United—Pray for a united world working for peace.

Unleash—Don't unleash your dog unless you know his or her bark is worse than their bite. Otherwise somebody may take a bite out of you with a lawsuit.

Unpopular—Don't let people bother you. You always have your own top fan you can count on: yourself.

Unreadable—Now if we could only read a doctor's writing, we could tell what kind of medicine we are going to be taking.

Unscramble—If we could unscramble some people's minds, we would have the cure of mental illness in many cases.

Unspoken—Some of the greatest words in the world are those words that aren't spoken.

Unused—If you have anything unused, use it. You'll be surprised what you can do with it.

Unworthy—Feeling unworthy is often the beginning of a downfall, so dispel this feeling as soon as possible.

Upbringing—Don't use upbringing as an excuse your sins. Take responsibility for yourself.

Upper Class—We are all upper class in God's mind.

Upset—Don't upset too many people. We need all the happiness we can get in this world.

Upstream—It doesn't matter if you go upstream or downstream, just that you are in the stream.

Uptight—Don't be uptight when a cool you would get the job done much better.

Use—Don't misuse people, for the doormat you use today may become the keyhole you have to go through tomorrow.

Useless—Nobody is useless. You are worth as much as you want to be.

Usher—Be considerate of them, because they serve so that you can enjoy.

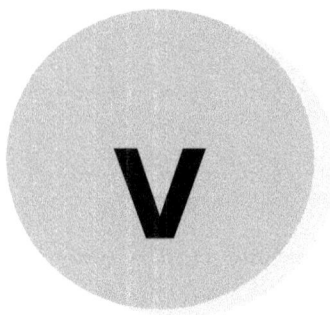

Vacancy—Develop your mind, otherwise you will have to put a vacancy sign on your head.

Vacation—When the pressure gets to be too much, take one.

Vacuum Cleaner—Be sure you vacuum your carpet, otherwise people will want to know how your crop is doing.

Valentine—Be one to somebody that will last a lifetime.

Valentine's Day—Show love everyday instead of just on Valentine's Day.

Valley—Don't get too depressed in life, because if you can survive the valleys, the mountaintops are yours.

Vandalism—Don't ruin the results of the hard work of others.

Vaudeville—It was good for what ailed you. Now the memories of it will have to serve your purpose, which isn't all bad.

Vault—You can store all the treasures you want in a vault, but the greatest treasure of all is the one stored in you. It is known as the heart. The love it can pour forth is priceless.

Veil—Don't live your life behind a veil. Come out of hiding.

Ventriloquist—Some marriages are like a ventriloquist: one mate does all the talking for the other mate. No wonder there are divorces in this world.

Venus—The goddess of love and beauty. If you find her, save her for a rainy day.

Verse—Write a verse to bring joy to others, not for the monetary value of it.

Very—Try to be very nice to somebody you don't like. The more hatred we conquer in this world, the more love we spread in its place.

Vest—A bulletproof vest is good, but a gun-less society is even better.

Veterans Day—Those who fought for freedom deserve this day to be thanked for the freedom they gave us.

Veterinarian—A good one sometimes friendlier and kinder than your family doctor.

Vice President—A lot of people say they can't remember the vice presidents. The vice presidents shouldn't feel bad. A lot of the presidents we remember, and we wish we didn't.

Vice Versa—Don't be vice versa so often that people call you the reversal kid.

Victim—Won't you be glad when you perpetrators of crime will be prosecuted instead of the victims?

Victory—Sometimes a loss can be your greatest victory. When you fall down, you have to get up and go on. When you go on, you have conquered defeat.

Vietnam—The men, women, and the children (yes, I said children) who fought in the Vietnam War did not lose the war. Anybody who fights for peace is not a loser. They are winners.

View—If you think the view from the top is great, you should see it from the bottom.

Viewpoint—Your viewpoint is important. Don't let any body tell you any different.

Vigor—Be vigorous in the morning, and you will be in charge of your life, and your goals will be obtainable.

Villain—What this person needs is a good guardian angel that can wing him a good one.

Violet—Buy some and give them to someone special in your life and become the violet of their heart.

Violin—Anybody who can play it has put years of practice into it, and they deserve all the applause you can give them.

Vision—Be the vision of peace for the rest of the world to see.

Visit—Visit those who are lonely.

Vitamin C—Take it and become the C kid on your block.

Vocabulary—It doesn't matter how big your vocabulary is, so long as people know what your message is. With some people, you have to carry a dictionary around just to look up the big words they use.

Voice—Raise your voice when it will make a difference to someone in need.

Volcano—Don't have such a bad temper that people wonder when your lava is going to spill over.

Volunteer—By lending a hand with your support, you could make a difference in somebody's life who has no spirit to go on.

Vote—Vote and know you did your part to keep America free.

Vulture—Some people are like this. When you are down and out, they really go to town on you.

Waddle—If you waddle like a duck, who cares, so long as you can walk and go where you want to.

Waffle Iron—Make a waffle for yourself; you deserve it.

Wagon Train—Don't knock it, because the pioneers traveled in it to form the kind of lifestyle you enjoy today.

Waiter—Smile when you wait on a table, because your smile might be the only friendly smile some people see all day.

Walk—When you walk at night, take a whistle along in case you need it.

Walk-on—A major part in a play, because you break up the boredom of the speaking parts.

Wallflower—It's all right to sit on the sidelines, but be sure to move once in a while so people know you are alive.

Walrus—I love them because they look so funny and they can bring a smile to anyone with a sad heart.

Waltz—Waltz to your heart's content. At least when you waltz you can tell you are dancing. Some of the other dances nowadays, the couples look like apes in heat.

Warmth—Be known for the warmth you spread, not the cold you never intend sometimes.

Warranty—This sometimes runs out before you get the product home from the store.

Wash—You can wash that man out of your hair, but you will need a strong rinse to get the memories out.

Wash and wear—With some clothes, this means being worn out after the first washing.

Washboard—A washboard sometimes cleans clothes better than some of the washing machines they make today.

Waste—They know how to do this in Washington.

Watch—Don't belittle a watch you get on retirement, because you know the hours of effort that you have accounted for. No company could ever repay an employee for the dedication you put forth.

Watchmaker—He or she uses his or her time to make your time.

Water—Save it, because without it we can't survive.

Watergate—They got caught with their hands in the cookie jar, and at the same time the door slammed on their behinds.

Wave—A friendly wave does make a difference to a depressed person.

Weak—Don't consider yourself a weak person, because everybody has strength that will show forth in due time.

Weather—Keep tabs on the weather, and you won't be caught short on a stormy day.

Weather-beaten—Some weathermen and weather vanes.

Weight—If the weight on your shoulders gets too heavy. Don't be afraid to ask for help. When you get back on your feet again, you can reestablish your goals.

Well-wisher—Wish everybody well, and the world will be well-off for you.

Whale—Save the whales, for God created them for people to enjoy, not to destroy.

Wheel—A lot of people think they are big wheels, but even a wheel stops when the brakes are put on.

Wheelchair—Some people in wheelchairs can do more than people who aren't, because where the body leaves off the mind takes over.

When—When are the roads easy to drive? In the winter it's snow and ice. In the summer it's potholes, road crews, and detours.

Wimp—Don't judge a book by its cover. We all have strength that will surface eventually.

Whip—Don't beat a child when talking would achieve greater results.

Whistle-stop—When small towns in America show their power in the election campaign.

White-collar—I's all right to dress grand, just make sure your output is as spectacular.

White Elephant—Take care of your white elephant, because it may be a precious elephant to someone else.

White House—Where the needs of the people are sometimes forgotten for one's own political gain.

Whitewash—Don't whitewash your mistakes, because once you start concealing you lose the sense of truth and your whole life becomes a concealment.

Wholehearted—Be sincere and full of energy when you do something, and you can cash in the dividends later on in life.

Wholesome—People who believe in God and sunshine are this.

Why—Don't ask why. Live life; don't try to understand it.

Widowhood—This may be a sad time, but don't forget, good moments lived are good memories left forever.

Wildcat—Be careful of a wildcat strike, because the company you work for might cut you down to a tame cat before it's over.

Wild-goose Chase—A wild-goose chase isn't so bad. Think of the exercise you get.

Wild Oats—Sow your wild oats, but don't forget they're yours come, the harvest time.

Will—Everybody has a will, build up a strong one so that when problems come in your way, you can stop them in their tracks.

Willingness—Express your willingness to help those in need when it occurs.

Wind-chill Factor—Too many politicians in a group.

Window—Anybody can slam a door in your face. Look for people who open windows. They can give you the break that you need in your life

Wine—Wine is to be enjoyed, not to pig out on

Wing—Spread your wings and be the lift people need in life.

Wink—Be careful you don't wink so much that you at tract the wrong kind of people.

Winning—Winning isn't everything, because once you get to the top of the ladder, you go down backwards, so humble yourself for the trip down

Wins—No matter who wins an election, you still have to go to work the next day. You have to earn your own keep, so don't let a politician make you believe you are going to get a free meal ticket when he or she gets into office.

Winter—Most people hate it, but when you survive it, you enjoy spring that much more.

Wise—If you are wise, share your wisdom with ochers for a more productive world.

Wish—Don't wish your life away. Do something positive for somebody, and you won't have time for wishing.

With—With love you can accomplish so much more in life.

Withdrawal—Don't withdraw into a corner. It is only through that we are alive.

Withhold—Don't withhold anything that will free the conscience of another person.

Witness—Be sure the facts you give are true, because it is only through truth that life progresses.

Witty—Make a sad world laugh, and laughter will be your battle cry.

Wizard—Pass your skills on and let others know the enjoyment of being clever.

Wolves—If some of your dinner guests eat like wolves, just provide shovels for them instead of silverware.

Womanhood—For some girls this happens early in their life. Some girls have no parent to guide them, so they must become the guides for themselves and maybe other siblings as well.

Wonder—It doesn't hurt to wonder about something. Curiosity doesn't kill the cat. It will make us more aware of where we are going.

Woodpecker—Don't be like this bird. Learn to do things quietly, and people won't mind having you around.

Wool—Enjoy it and be kind to the sheep that provided it.

Word—If you give a speech, abbreviate your words and make them to the point. People appreciate this more than a windmill running off at the mouth, saying nothing comprehensive.

Work—Work and no play will tire you, but all play and no work will make you a lazy son of a gun.

Workhorse—If you are one, make sure you are getting the pay you deserve.

Workout—Do enough exercise, and you can live the kind of life you want to live.

World—God didn't make an awful world. He made a beautiful one. It is some of the people living in it that make it awful. Let's not allow them to do it. Do your part to spread all the goodness and kindness you can.

Worldwide—Taking care of worldwide hunger is fine, but don't forget about local hunger.

Worry—Don't worry about anything. Take one day at a time, and you will make it through life with flying colors.

Worship—Worship God, not the ground that somebody walks on.

Worthy—Make sure you are worthy of the praise given to you, because then you will feel so much better accepting it.

Wrap—If you see the next person's troubles and you see how small yours are, maybe you can wrap yours up and be done with them.

Wrap Up—Wrap up your life with goodness, and you will wipe our evil on your own accord.

Wreath—Remember your loved ones who have passed on by putting a wreath on their graves on Christmas and Memorial Day.

Wreck—If you look into a mirror and see this, do something about it, because only you can help yourself.

Wren—Don't forget to feed the birds in the winter. If you have a birdbath and an afford it, buy a water heater for it.

Wriggle—Don't try to wriggle your way out of something. Take responsibility for your actions.

Wringer—Wring out your troubles, and you will see just how small they are.

Wrinkle—Wrinkles don't have to spoil your life. Just think of them as the stars you have won in the battle of life.

Write Off—Don't write off anything. Hope is so much better.

Wrong—If you are proven wrong, accept it and go on from there, vowing to do the right thing whenever possible.

Wronged—People talk about getting even. Why stoop to the level of the person or persons who wronged you? Just be thankful you don't have to live up to their consciences.

X—The letter X isn't used much, but without it there would be an empty place between W and Y.

Xerox—They copy the world and bring it closer together everyday.

X-rated—There must be a demand for X-rated movies, because otherwise they wouldn't be on the market. The day they don't make any money, they will go off the market.

X-ray—Take one of your life and see if everything is clear. If not, do what you have to do to make it clear.

Xylophone—A beautiful instrument to listen to. Anybody who has learned it has put a lot of practice into it.

Yacht—Your boat may not be a yacht, but at least you can sail it.

Yard—Yard work is healthy for you. If you are able to do it, do it.

Yardage—If you think your progress with something is too slow, remember, yards are made by an inch.

Yardstick—Measure your life by how much good you do instead of how much money you make.

Yawn—Don't open your mouth so wide that the whole Russian army can march through it.

Year—It used to be "who will care in a hundred years?" Today it is more like, "who will care tomorrow?"

Yearbook—So what if you aren't in your high school yearbook. If you graduate, the mark you have is far greater than the picture you don't.

Yearling—Take care of this, and when it grows up, you will have the prized animal you want.

Yearn—May all the good things you wish for come true.

Yeast—May all your expectations rise to the degree you desire.

Yell—If you are ever in a situation where you need help, yell. Don't do it, though, if it will endanger your life. Pray silently if you can't yell for help.

Yellow—Yellow is supposed to be the color of a coward, but let it be the beauty you want it to be.

Yellow Pages—Use them if your eyes and fingers can walk better than your legs.

Yesterday—Your yesterdays can live on forever through the memories of today.

Yiddish—If you can speak it, don't be ashamed to use it.

Yield—Don't be afraid to give in if somebody else is right. If light is produced, what difference does it make who produces it?

Yodel—Display the e great talent God gave you and entertain people who are lonely and need an uplift in their lives. A nursing home would be a great start.

Yoga—Good exercise if you can do it.

Yom Kippur—A beautiful Jewish holiday. Let's hope the prayers offered during Yom Kippur bring peace to the Holy Land.

You—You are important, because nobody can be you better than you can.

Young—Young at heart is the only age meter that counts.

Yourself—Be yourself, not somebody else. Excel at being yourself. Don't try to copy anyone. Variety provides more fun in life than sameness.

Yummy—Be thankful for the tasty food grown in America.

Zebra—A zebra has stripes, but that doesn't make it a coward.

Zero—If your team has a score of zero after a game, don't feel bad. When you try hard, that is the only thing that counts.

Zest—Develop a gusto for life and pass it on.

Zigzag—If you are doing chis while driving a car, pull over to the side of the road and wait for help to arrive.

Zip Code—Don't let numbers make you forget the name of your town.

Zipper—An idea Xmas gift for a talkative person.

Zodiac—No matter what your sign is, live your life from the strength from within, and you will make it through the night.

Zone—Everybody is born equal, so don't divide people by specific restrictions.

Zoo—Some places of work are like this and there is some resemblance to the animals.

Zoology—Study animals and help provide the best environment possible for them.

www.ingramcontent.com/pod-product-compliance
Lightning Source LLC
Chambersburg PA
CBHW041624140626
46547CB00030B/846